SOMERSET
TALES OF A PASSER BY

Is dedicated to the late Graham Watts who wanted to share his fond memories.

Graham's Family would like to thank everyone who has helped create this book in honour of a very special man.

Illustrations by Molly Butler.

Book design by Chauncey Gardner.

Printed by Book Printing UK www.bookprintinguk.com

Remus House, Coltsfoot Drive, Peterborough, PE2 9BF

Printed in Great Britain

ISBN 978-1-3999-9059-2

CONTENTS

Graham with his walking companion Luna.

FOREWARD

Graham as a young boy.

Graham was born in rural Somerset just after the end of World War Two. The youngest of five children, he grew up knowing that he wanted to follow in his farming father's footsteps. As a young boy, he saw little point in bothering with history, literature, or other academic subjects; after all, what could they teach him that he had not already learned from the people and the countryside around him?

As an adult he became a successful farmer and later an agricultural contractor, widely involved within his community and always maintaining his early Somerset links. He hoped that local people might find it interesting to read about his childhood memories of growing up at Wellesley Farm and raising his own family there, before retiring in the nearby village of North Wootton.

Retirement brought reflection and he wrote about his fond childhood memories, sharing them with the local villagers through the monthly publication of The North Wootton News.

In all, he moved only a few miles from his birthplace to the place he came to rest but his experience and knowledge was second to none and despite his aversion to history and English lessons, he had a natural gift for bringing a fast disappearing way of life to a very wide audience.

He often expressed that maybe 'others' would be interested in his stories and after a lifetime of raising funds for various charities, his family have compiled this book in his memory to raise money for The Dorset & Somerset Air Ambulance.

His sudden death has deprived us all of the chance to enjoy more Somerset gems from A Passer By...

A day out at Dorset Steam Show.

A BOY AND AN UNUSUAL FIRE ALARM

When I was a boy we did not have mains electricity, not many houses did. We would visit my uncle who farmed at Wincanton, his lighting was provided by several pump pressurized paraffin lamps, they gave out an impressive bright light and of course heat as a bonus. In fact, my uncle said that when mains electric was brought to the farm, they missed the heat in the house that the lamps provided.

Anyway, back home we did have electric lights and all that comes with the advantages of electricity, the only difference was that this electric came from a farm generator, no Hinkley Point in those days. Actually, Hinkley Point was there, the power station wasn't, or the pylons on the Levels come to that!

Dad's generator was a fine piece of modern engineering no need to swing the starting handle to start it, all you had to do was to switch on a light or plug in an appliance and the engine would automatically start up and supply power. When the light or appliance was switched off the power plant would shut down, that was the theory anyway. This of course meant you couldn't have electric freezers or fridges that we take for granted today.

This was all very convenient but had its down side's, sometimes dad, who usually went to bed last, would switch off his bedroom light and the power plant would continue to run, which meant somewhere on the farm someone had left a light burning. Dad would have to get up, search for the offending light and switch it off, the generator would then shut down. However, would this inconvenience later save the farm from disaster?

In my younger days the variety of cleaning chemicals were not available and dad used Sodium Carbonate Decahydrate as a dairy cleaner. This chemical is still readily available today known as Sodium Crystals from your local store, I can recommend it to you all, for those difficult cleaning jobs, especially the barbecue (however I digress.) Dad used to supplement this cleaning agent with hot steam to remove what we call 'milk fats'. If milk fats are not removed from the inside surface of milk pipes on a regular basis it would build up and would cause the milk to go sour. The steam was provided by a big coal fired boiler situated as close as possible to the dairy building. I spent many an hour sat next to that boiler as a child especially in Winter, and all around in the boiler house were hanging lots of old army great coats, being aired, these were worn by the farm labourers. Sometimes the boiler was not efficient, and dad would say, I bet that coal delivered from the agent is not the best Welsh steam coal. It appeared in those days, that the best steam coal from Wales was reserved for the railways.

One night dad went to bed, switched off his light and the electric plant shut down, all was peaceful.

Dad recalled that he had been asleep about an hour when the electric plant started up, so who was out there switching on lights? He had to get up and go off on his rounds to find who or what was responsible, and what he discovered was not an intruder or light bulb burning but the roof of the farm barn was ablaze. To cut a long story short, the fire brigade from Wells were soon on parade and the fire was put out, but not until significant damage was caused to the barn roof.

Graham with his father
Sydney Thomas (Tom) Watts.

The investigation was carried out, and it was thought that a spark from the farm steam boiler had alighted the barn roof, and the burning of the light cable on the beams created the short cut that started the generator.

I remember my Dad saying: "if it was not for that generator making me get out of bed, we could have lost the Farm".

Thankful Times.

A Passer By.

A BOY AND A SUMMER

As I rode my old bike up the farm lane, I could hear the sound of the old Lister D engine, the smell of hot water and oil and the clatter of the slats on the hay elevator and I knew that Dad's hay was being collected and placed in a rick constructed in the corner of the hay field.

The rick when completed would be thatched with reed straw to make it waterproof, the contents of the rick would be fed to the cows in the winter months and a small rail fence would be constructed around the rick to stop the cows from attacking it until it was required.

It all began with the mowing. This was carried out by the skilled tractor driver who Dad employed. Although he was a general farm labourer, tractor driving was his main employment and he was a very skilled man. The mowing was done with an old horse drawn mower that had been adapted and converted so that it could be pulled by the tractor, this machine had a reciprocating knife that had to be sharpened at regular intervals, so several blades were taken to the field so that it could be changed if the original blade got blunt or part of the blade went missing.

This mower had what was called a swath board attached at the end of the blade housing, it was constructed out of a solid plank of elm or ash and to everyone's annoyance it would snap off if you forgot to raise the cutting bar prior to reversing when in work. This happened often and the local suppliers must have sold dozens of these in a cutting season.

Graham asleep on Hessian sacking after a tiring day.

If the weather was fine then after several days the grass would require to be turned over so that it would dry on the other side. Dad had an Alice Chalmers petrol paraffin tractor and it was quite small but had a double seat and we kids were allowed to drive it accompanied by an adult. It was attached to what was called a Dickie hay turner and after instructions from Dad or the tractor driver, we were allowed to turn the hay. You had to be very careful and drive accurately and slowly or the hay would not be completely tuned over, and if that happened it would take longer to dry, and that could be a disaster especially if the weather was what we called catchy.

When I was very small the ricks were constructed in what is called loose hay, which basically meant that it was not baled up as it is today, the loose hay when dry would be swept by a swath turner into what was called windrows, and it was then pulled up into large piles by a large mechanical hay rake.

An apparatus called a hay sweep which looked a bit like a giant hair comb was attached to the front axle of the tractor, no hydraulic attachment in those days. The large piles of hay were then individually pushed to the hay rick, if the ground was full of hollows sometimes the tines would push into the ground and break off.

Threshing in The Paddock at Wellesley Farm.

Some farmers used old cars and trucks to attach the sweep, I think the idea was to speed up the operation; however, it could only be as efficient as the labourers who had to pitch or roll the hay into the elevator by hand at the rick site.

The foundations of the rick were constructed from limbs cut from oak trees; these were placed on the ground to elevate the hay from the damp soil, and constructed to what size you estimated you would require.

Once the hay was in the elevator it was deposited onto the rick, it was then placed by hand around the rick, we kids often had to run around the surface to consolidate the hay especially on the corners, as the rick construction progressed so the elevator was raised using a hand winch to a higher position.

It may sound a bit dangerous but like I have said before, we were taught that the work place was not a playground and it was the education we received as youngsters from Dad and the labourers that steered us away from danger. It was a working farm environment, and we were aware of it.

Sometimes if the hay was not completely dry when the rick was constructed, it would heat up to the extent that it would catch fire due to what is called spontaneous combustion. There used to be an old saying: Make it in May and it will catch fire in August. To see if the rick was heating, Dad had this long metal spike which was pushed into the centre, there it was left for about an hour, after that it was withdrawn and checked to see how hot it had become. If it was deemed to be too hot - and you could smell that it was hot - then something had to be done and quickly or you would have a disaster on your hands. Dad had this piece of apparatus; it was like a round cylindrical cutter about six inches in diameter, attached to this cutter was a long metal shaft with a wooden turning handle, the idea was to cut a hole through the rick to allow air to flow through and cool it down.

When I was about 8 years old, Dad bought a hay baler and the job of clearing a field of hay and constructing a rick was a lot easier and quicker. The hay ricks disappeared when Dad purchased and had constructed a corrugated tin domed roofed hay barn.

This particular barn was manufactured and prefabricated by a company called Bolton and Paul, they came from up north somewhere, they sent down a team of construction workers to dig the footings and bolt it all together. However, after the first day the workers failed to return to the farm from their accommodation somewhere in Wells. Work came to a standstill. Then, Dad had a phone call from Wells Police Station to enquire if Dad would go in and pay the bail money so they could be released from the police cells where they had been incarcerated after they all got drunk and had been arrested after an affray. The bond was paid, the men released, and Dad finally managed to get the barn finished.

To me as a child the haymaking season was my favourite time of year, long hot sunny days, and that lovely smell of freshly cut grass as it slowly dried out, a busy time when extra labour came to the farm to help gather it all in before the rains came. The picnics in the field when Mum brought out baskets of food and tea for all the seasonal workers, this was always appreciated by all.

So, there you are, just some of my memories of the old days of haymaking on a Somerset dairy farm.

A time I enjoyed and will always remember.

A Passer By.

A BOY AND A DONKEY

When I was a small boy, if people asked what I wanted to be when I grew up, I would say I wanted to be a cowboy, not because of the fact that I grew up with cows and saw my future with them, but I think it was more to do with the influence of all the cowboy films that I watched on television.

These film series came on at least twice a week, they starred well-known characters like Roy Rogers, Kit Carson, The Lone Ranger, Hop Along Cassidy, The Cisco Kid, and his sidekick Pancho and many more whose names I can no longer remember. They were always portrayed in black and white as colour television had not yet been invented.

It is rather strange thinking back, that these guys never actually herded cows. They were always rescuing stage coaches from Indian attackers or chasing masked bandits after the pay roll that always seemed to be at risk.

They were the good guys, pillars of society, always on the right side of the law and our heroes. They roamed the range on their beautiful horses, sat square in the saddle not bouncing up and down like the

huntsmen that rode in their European style across Dad's land in the hunting season.

My brothers and I spent hours playing Cowboys and Indians, all on foot as we did not have horses to ride. What we needed were horses, three if we could get them, one each.

There were no horses on our farm, they had been replaced by tractors many years before, although Uncle Burt who farmed in Dulcote still had a large mare and putt which he used to feed the cows in the fields in winter, he would say to Dad: "See, I have not made any marks in my field, not like you churning up your turf with that ruddy tractor and trailer." However back to my story about donkeys.

We harped on to Dad that we wanted some horses and he would say: "We got enough ruddy animals to feed now, without bringing

horses back on the farm". This was a big disappointment to us kids who longed to imitate our western heroes. Also, I don't think he wanted to part with his money, good horses were not cheap.

In the end a compromise was found. Dad knew this guy who kept donkeys that were employed to give kids' rides on Weston-Super-Mare beach, apparently at the end of the summer season he would allow the donkeys to go on holiday to local farms for the winter. Dad agreed that we could winter one donkey. So, the day arrived and the large cattle trailer was hitched to the land-rover and we were off, full of excitement to collect our donkey.

Dad drove onto the beach to be met by a very happy beach trader who, on realising that there were three kids looking excitedly through the land-rover windows, he had the opportunity to off load three donkeys into our care. Before Dad could object, the man had three donkeys complete with saddles and tack safely stowed in his trailer. This guy had obviously done this many times before to previous gullible farmers.

On arrival back at the farm, the donkeys were unloaded into the old cart shed that Dad had converted into make shift stable accommodation with lots of warm straw to lay on and a crib full of Dad's best hay, these animals I'm sure, thought they had arrived in paradise.

The first job to do was to groom and de-lice them. Next their feet had to be trimmed because the fact that they lived on the beaches, the sand did not wear down their hooves and as a result it look like they were wearing football boots.

First expense for Dad was a visit from the vet with his cutters and files; Dad said that ruddy owner knew what he was doing when he fobbed us off with those blinking beasts. However, to us kids it was all a great adventure, learning all about donkey welfare, all very much like looking after cattle, the only difference being these three were obstinate and very crafty.

Trying to put on their saddles was a trial in itself, we kids couldn't do it as they used to blow up their stomachs and it was impossible to do up the girth, so an adult had to come and punch them in the stomach to make them breathe out; once this was achieved it was simple. I think the donkeys saw this as some sort of inherited game.

So, there we were all lined up in the home paddock, the donkeys with the bit between their teeth and us boys in the saddles, donkeys well fed and groomed to perfection, nothing now to stop us from riding our imaginary range and rescue the postman on his GPO bike from imaginary mail thieves.

A nice tap on their backsides from Mother with her washing tongs and we were away on a great adventure. Well, we thought so, but about a hundred yards from the homestead, the donkeys turned and raced back to the stable. Mother came down after us and found all three cowboys sat in the saddle while those crafty devils filled their stomachs with dad's best hay.

Dad explained to us that this could be an ongoing problem as the donkeys only had to walk up and down the beach for a short distance to satisfy the punter who partook of donkey rides.

So again, a compromise had to be made, the donkeys were quite happy to roam the range as long as the range was one hundred yards that way and a hundred yards this way, they would keep this up all day but go in one direction more than that, the hell they would!

We had great fun with the donkeys but I must admit that the novelty wore off long before the winter was over and so they had a great winter holiday roaming the fields by day, not being pestered by kids and feasting on Dad's best hay at night in their warm snug stable.

All too soon their holiday was over and we knew that they were beginning to miss the kids and their fellow donkeys that were already back on the beach as the new season had started.

We missed them when they went home but Dad was a wise old bird, he knew we had to get horses out of our system, and we did. It was probably a good idea that he did not buy us horses as I believe, like the donkeys the novelty would have worn off and Dad would have been stuck with three unwanted horses.

Home and on the Range.

A Passer By.

A BOY AND A CHRISTMAS

Today the run up to and the advertising of Christmas starts around the end of September, long before the clocks take us from summer to autumn and winter. It's probably all to do with advertising and the pre-Christmas sales expectation of the multi-national companies who now supply us with a very commercial Christmas, and we are all daft enough to go along with and encourage them.

I was in a store in Weston in mid-September and there it was, a Christmas tree along with all its tacky Chinese imported decorations, accompanied by a nodding polar bear. I enquired to a lady assistant was she aware that the clocks would not change for another month and her reply was: "well, we noticed that the shop down the road had a tree, so we thought we had better put out ours." It has almost become an obsession to see who can be the first to install a fully decorated Christmas tree and play merry tunes on the speaker systems - talk about ruddy sheep!

When I was a boy some 60 years ago it was all so different, no television adverts suggesting if you don't buy that 'said' toy in October it wouldn't be available in December, or adverts dropping through your door, saying 'buy this new furniture for Christmas now and pay for it in 3 years' time, and then only if you can afford it!'

Today by the time it's Christmas week we are all sick and tired of it and only want it over with as painlessly as possible, but I guess that would only be an adult's opinion. Kids still see it as the most exciting time of year. At this point in my story, I feel like Charles Dickens' character, Scrooge!

I suppose thinking about it, when we were children the thought of preparing for Christmas did raise its head at home in late October, not through adverts or sales propaganda but through the order mum gave to Ways and Co's sales rep: these included raisins and currants and all the ingredients needed to manufacture several Christmas puddings.

Mum would mix together all the ingredients needed including a few six penny pieces in a large porcelain bowl, all by hand with a large wooden spoon. It must have been hard work. Once prepared it was dispensed into several large basins, the tops of which were sealed with a muslin cloth tied with string. Then she would place two large bricks in this huge aluminium vessel, fill it with a given amount of water and place the puddings on top of the bricks, then put on the lid and place on the AGA cooker there to steam away until they were cooked.

The puddings were cooled then placed in a larder until served at Christmas dinner and at every dinner in January until they were all consumed. No way would they been thrown out in those days.

It was around Wells' carnival time that we kids really started to think about the toy that we would like to have from Mum and Dad and by this time the shops were full of all sorts of toys. The Chisholm sisters had a large toy shop in Wells and this was the favourite shop for us kids, we didn't always get what we wanted but we were never disappointed in what was given.

I remember one year I was given a clockwork train set that went round and round on metal rails in a continuous circle until it needed rewinding. It was always a favourite and I remember it was made of tin and you could slice an apple on the sharp edges of the carriages. It was also possible that it was painted with lead paint. We played with this toy always, and I can't remember ever being cut or poisoned, but this type of toy was later banned under health and safety rules, along with unsecure eyes in teddy bears - probably for the best. Years later I found part of the track in the old cheese room at the back of the Farm House. That train set would be a collector's item today.

Cowboy guns were always a favourite with caps made with a small amount of gun powder which when fed through the gun mechanism to make them sound life-like when the trigger was pulled.

In the early years of my childhood there wasn't any Christmas type wrapping paper and all our gifts were wrapped in thick brown paper and tied up with string with a nice bow that we kids could undo.

On Christmas Eve, we would hang up a sock each on the

shelf above the AGA and early to bed all full of excitement and anticipation. The Christmas tree that was dug up from the garden that afternoon was brought into the house but we were not allowed to decorate it, or decorate the rooms in the house.

Next morning, we awoke early even before Dad had got up to milk the cows, to find the rooms of the house all decorated and the tree in its chosen place in the dining room all decorated with its little fairy on the top that never changed all the years we were young. We rushed downstairs and opened our respective toys, and retrieved the contents of our stockings with the same expectation as kids do today, although the apples and oranges in our stockings were not the computers, laptops or mobile phones expected today - they had not been invented, but we always had a new pocket knife which was useful for cutting bale strings and opening feed bags. You imagine the outcry if kids had knives given to then today, they would all be arrested for carrying offensive weapons - different times - different mentality.

It was Christmas on a farm and like it or not the farm chores still had to be done, the cows still had to be milked and the calves fed and we kids had to do our share. Dad used to double feed the cows on Christmas Eve to lessen the work on Christmas Day.

After dinner we would sit by the fire for an hour or so and eat small oranges, and I will always remember that delicious smell of citrus that came from the peel as it dried out in the hearth in front of the fire. Then, it was put on your boots and let's get the farm chores done as soon as we can: even so it was usually about 5.30 pm before we came back into the house.

Mum would have prepared a large supper and usually would have invited friends or neighbours to join us, with large hams and joints of meat to be carved and presented on the table, along with Christmas crackers. It was a large banquet but as we had all been out working in the afternoon, we all had huge appetites and did the meal justice. This was followed by chocolate log, trifles, and chocolate tea cakes, the only time in the year when we did. The adults consumed beer, cider and wine and always seemed to get happier and louder as the night went on.

The candles on the Christmas tree were lit, they were made of wax and had a real flame, and we would sit and admire this magnificent sight. Years later we thought how dangerous this had been but at the time seemed harmless enough.

Merry Times.

(May I take this opportunity to wish you all a Merry Christmas, and prosperous New Year.)

A Passer By.

A BOY AND AN INDIAN CAMP

As small kids we attended Coxley Primary School. This was due to the geographical location where we grew up. I think Wootton School and Dinder School were closer but we came under St Cuthbert's Out Parish, so Coxley School under the Head of Miss Blackwell was the base of our primary education.

The majority of pupils who attended Coxley School were like ourselves, the offspring of parents who farmed or whose occupations where in some way closely attached to the agricultural prosperity of the countryside. One year, it was around 1956, a number of young Hungarian refugees arrived at the school and we kids had to help teach them the English language. Dad said it was to do with the Hungarian Civil War and something about the Russian army, but we were too young to understand what it was all about. However, I will always remember those frightened unhappy children and I like to think and hope, that our welcome and friendship towards them in some way eased their plight.

Graham and his brothers Richard and Peter enjoying camp life.

My brothers and I had lots of friends at school and my older brothers' friends became mentors to us younger ones educating us on nature and the wildlife that abounded the countryside, they also assisted us in repairing punctures and breakdowns on our bikes which seemed to blight all our adventures.

On most Saturdays lots of our school friends would cycle over to the farm to play, but of course we had to complete our farm chores first. With lots of help from our mates these were soon accomplished. If lots of kids appeared, Dad would use this opportunity to move cattle around the farm, "many hands make light work," he would say, "and you will still have plenty of time for play later."

On one occasion we loaded our bikes onto Dad's truck and he drove us to Priddy Hill Farm which was located about 2 miles away. Well, it was our job to race ahead and overtake the animals and stand in open gateways or farm entrances to prevent the cows from straying. Dad followed on in the truck to bring up the rear. This involved bringing them through the centre of Wells, but not so many cars about in those days. It took us all morning to arrive back at the farm, but what an adventure for us kids and our mates although, after this epic journey we were all too tired to play.

Above the farm was a wood of about 30 hectares with bluebells and wild garlic, it was the perfect adventure ground for the 20 or more kids who used to play there.

One day it was decided that we would build a camp to play in, we used to play cowboys and Indians a lot and after some discussion it was decided that it was to be an Indian Camp, although I must admit as I remember it, not many of us wanted to be Indians as the cowboys always seemed to win.

So, an Indian camp it was to be and we set about it with gusto and great enthusiasm. It was large and took us about three weekends to complete, however as news of the camp spread through school, it was decided we would let other kids join us, as long as they were prepared to be Indians!! It then took us the time to commence building the number of tepee's required.

We were all country lads so every one of us had a sheath knife or pen knife, also kids raided their dads' shed for saws and hatchets or any other useful tools. Young saplings were cut to make and provide the tent poles, these we lashed together with baler twine the supply of which on the farm was in abundance, these in turn were covered in old Hessian sacks again procured from the farm. We built about 6 of these structures.

The completion of the camp took many weekends but created great fun and entertainment for all who took part. I have to say at this time our tribe had grown to large proportions, all our friends wanted to be involved, some kids rode their bikes all the way up from Godney laden down with materials for construction.

Thinking back, it was during accomplishments such as the building of the camp that created a kind of bonding and friendship between kids that lasts a lifetime and after 60 years I still reminisce with my old chums of the time we built the camp. Somehow, I don't see how kids can gain that sort of comradeship that lasts a lifetime from Facebook or media trash that the kids play with today. In the end we all took it in turns to be the Indians defending the camp, as the cowboys crept up through the undergrowth to try and capture its occupants.

Graham and his brothers
Richard and Peter.

It's hard to believe that we used bows and arrows to attack and defend, also we used spears which we actually threw at one another and sometimes it would all get out of hand. You would see one batch of kids chasing another batch of kids out of the wood and down across the fields to the sanctuary of the Rancher's house, where refreshments where made available to all combatants. After the battles we were always covered in mud, blood and tears but by God we had some fun.

Sometimes the Indians and the cowboys would congregate in the camp and agree a peace treaty for the weekend and we would build a large open fire and cook potatoes in the hot coals which we ate with gusto along with, I'm sure, a peck of dirt. The camp took a decline as we all moved on to senior school and not so much time on our hands, especially after we saved up and bought an old motorcycle which we rode around the fields and the playing of cowboys and Indians became part of our own history.

Many years later when I had children of my own, I was up in the wood and rediscovered the dilapidated site of our camp that nature was taking back as her own, I sat for a while on an old log, forgot all about business problems and the trials of life and for a while I was back with my mates attacking and defending the old camp.

I think it's a shame that kids are not allowed any more to go into woods and build Indian camps, society would be much better off if they could.

Joys of Mates and the countryside.

A Passer By.

A BOY AND A LESSON TO BE LEARNT

Once every week, the instructions were: Come on, stop doodling and get yourself changed or you will be late for Sunday School.

These were the words I dreaded as a child: why would Mum think that I would enjoy being shut up in some old church room and being instructed about God and his creation when I was already growing up and experiencing the enjoyment of life in his world creation in the countryside of Somerset, especially when it was summer!

Not allowed to play on the lawn with my brothers, or go to play in the woods with our mates on Sunday afternoons? No! we had to go to ruddy Sunday School.

So, with Mum waving us off from the farmhouse kitchen window, we set off to walk to the church rooms at Dulcote, about one mile away, there to be met by our cousins who were also dragging their feet forwards as they were about as enthusiastic as we were.

The school room/chapel was and still is a pleasant attractive building. It was constructed and maintained as a village parochial chapel school room, by the generosity of Mrs M C

Graham with his mother, brothers and Aunt Ivy on a Sunday school trip to Weymouth.

Tudway, who paid for its construction back in 1860. It could accommodate about 60 children although I doubt there were ever that many kids in the village at that time.

The chapel was established in connection with St Cuthbert's Out parish, Wells and could seat about a hundred parishioners, it did not have its own vicar but had a circuit minister. I don't know what happened if you died back then, as far as I know there is no graveyard at the chapel, or in the village. However, back to my story.

We climbed up the flight of steps to the church room and entered through the large oak door, there to be met by a student from the Wells Ecclesiastical College whose duty it was to hold the lesson. These young men were very pleasant, always made us welcome and always had interesting stories to tell to us from the New Testament.

Our attendance was recorded and to prove to our parents that we had actually attended, we were given colourful stamps depicting a subject from the Bible that we had to stick in a little book which we were all given when we started the term. I'm sure these students who were very talented went on to great achievements within the church vocation they had chosen. I wonder if any of them are alive today?

I must admit they could not hold my attention for long and my mind would drift off to other more interesting topics as to how were the cows and dogs getting on while we were away, or would Dad's hay become fit to bale that afternoon?

The most exciting time of year was the Sunday School annual trip to the seaside, this was usually at Weymouth and was accessed via Mr Bond's rickety old coach, that rumbled, groaned, screeched, and sometimes boiled its way through the county's narrow roads to finally arrive with all occupants hot and bothered at the (Swannery) car park. With all the other kids and Mums, we arrived at the beach with deck chairs for the oldies to sit on.

We kids sat on towels which were also used to dry us after leaving the sea we were always a bit sore after being vigorously

dried by an enthusiastic aunt who didn't realise or didn't care that the towel was full of sand.

A banquet was prepared on the large blankets laid out on the sand, the food in abundance, which usually came from numerous large OXO tins which were used as storage and of course hot tea from large vacuum flasks, all topped off with lots of ice cream, which to us kids was indeed a luxury. We all played in harmony on the sand, large sand castles to be made, with moats that numerous kids with buckets of sea water carried yards could not fill.

A Punch and Judy show was watched with the usual untiring enthusiasm and then it was time to pack up, count the kids to make sure none were missing and then embark on the homeward journey. I don't think many of us remembered the homeward journey as we were all asleep before the coach left the outskirts of Weymouth, exhausted from a good day's activity, and the sea air. However back to Sunday School.

One afternoon it was decided as a group that we were not going to attend, so with the agreement of our cousins we headed off for a walk on Dulcote Hill. It was a lovely afternoon in summer we had great fun rolling down the hill when we should have been taking religious instruction. I'm afraid the church did not stand a chance that day. Instead, nature won our hearts and attention, I think we told Mum that the student hadn't turned up so went for a walk instead, I never did know if she found out the truth.

On another occasion I pretended that I was unwell and certainly could not walk to Dulcote, let alone attend the Sunday School. I watched with glee from my bedroom window as my brothers headed away from the farm, but to my horror when they returned from the meeting they told me that Jesus was there and he wondered why I had not come to see him! Well, I can tell you I was devastated at the news, that I had missed the chance to meet Jesus in the flesh and vowed that I would attend Sunday school every week from then on just in case Jesus would return, but of course he never did.

I'm not a religious man but I have faith and I am a God-fearing man, but I don't need to go to church to prove it. I hold the view that it's the parents' responsibility to have their children christened, but it must be left up to the teenager to decide if they wish to be confirmed. So, who knows, with the faith I do have, maybe, there will be a chance to meet up with Jesus one day, I like to think so.

The Day I learnt a Lesson.

A Passer By.

A BOY AND A BIRD

It was at school one day that one of my chums who lived on a farm at Westbury-Sub-Mendip told me that he had a pet Jackdaw.

My friend Jim explained how he had obtained his new pet, how he had reared it and the enjoyment that owning such a unique pet had brought into his young life. I thought that was really cool, so that Saturday I took my bicycle and rode down to Jim's farm to see the bird and gain some more information as I was determined to own a pet Jackdaw of my own. The following spring, I was out and about the farm in search of a pair of breeding birds, I knew they nested in hollow trees so that's where I concentrated my search.

My uncle Tom owned the neighbouring field to Dad's and in the hedge abounding the road was an old hollow pollard oak tree. Now, a pollard oak is a normal oak tree that has had its branches removed over the years to provide fence posts and fire wood, this encourages the tree to produce many more branches. These trees usually have a very short trunk but numerous branches. There is a very good example on Blenheim's Hill. However, I digress from my Story.

As I mentioned Uncle Tom's Tree was hollow so an obvious place to commence my search and the trunk as it was being, it was easy to climb. On further investigation I discovered an active nest with two eggs, and as a bonus it was within the limited length of my short arms. So, the scene was set, all I had to do was to keep it under observation until the fledglings where grown but not yet ready to leave the security of the nest.

The day arrived and I removed one of the fledglings and transferred it into a hay lined box, this was to become its new home, until it could fly - you could say it was a "Jack in the Box"!

I fed my new pet on bread mixed with warm milk, quite different to its normal diet, but it grew with the utmost vigour and the day arrived when it was ready to meet the outside world. I have to say at this stage that my mum and dad where somewhat bemused by my activities but tolerated it when I cuddled Jack in the house. I never did know what its gender was but what else could you call a Jackdaw?

So, the day arrived when Jack was to be released, would he fly away or hang around? I knew he was a creature of the wild and would make his own choice. Well as you guessed, he decided to hang around and became a great favourite with everybody on the farm. Jack would always come to you if you called his name, even if you could not see where he was, he would appear, fly down to you and sit on your arm.

As I mentioned he was a creature of the wild so had complete freedom. Jack did his own thing and I`m sure he had many adventures, especially as we had farm dogs and farm cats that had to be avoided.

When I cycled home from school Jack would spot me coming up the lane and would fly down and sit on my shoulder, which was fine but, he couldn't always control his bowels.

Reps would arrive at the farm and if the car window was open Jack would fly down and land in the rep's lap, perhaps he thought a car was a mobile hollow tree!

Mum took us on holiday, so I wasn't around to feed Jack and I was a bit worried how he would survive the week I was away, although Jack was a wild creature, he came to me to be fed. I couldn't rely on Dad as he always referred to Jack as that Bloody Bird.

However, on arriving home Jack was still alive and well, on enquiring to Dad if he had fed Jack he told me he had not, but not to worry as that "Bloody Bird" had got into mother's larder during our vacation and eaten all the Cream Crackers and Dad said: "who taught him how to open the biscuit tin?"

I could go on and on with tales of Jack, but have limited space, only to say that one day he was missing, all the calling of a young child, did not return him.

Dad said perhaps he went off with one of the reps or maybe he had got into the wrong car and had been taken away, it was nice to see that even he was concerned over the safety of that Bloody Bird.

I saw my Friend Jim and told him of the fate that had become of Jack, and Jim said: "Guess what? my bird managed to drown itself in the cow trough last week."

Sad Days.

A Passer By.

A BOY AND AN ORCHARD

Down by the side of the old farmhouse next to where Grandad used to garage his Austin Seven car, was an object that to us kids looked like an old wild west stage coach, although the wheels were too small. The bulk of the machine made up for this deficiency, so we climbed aboard and rode the range for hours, pretending we had a team of fine horses in harness to race us across the Prairie.

Mother was always afraid that we would fall off and hurt ourselves but we never did, apart from a well-deserved bruise or two awarded whilst defending the stage coach from Indian borderers.

This machine was large in proportion, it had two spiked rollers and two large stone rollers built into its mechanism and a huge flywheel connected to a shaft protruding from its side, complete with a huge fly wheel. It was a well-engineered piece of equipment. Some of our older readers may well have recognised that what I have described in short detail, is in fact an old apple mill, built around about 1905.

It was powered by a running belt that ran from the flywheel to a pulley on the tractor and before tractors, possibly a steam engine. As its name suggests it was used to crush apples, in fact tons of apples, to convert the apples to what is called apple pumas which I'm sure you all know is the main ingredient for making that famous Somerset drink - Cider.

The apple pumas was collected into a large tub that sat underneath and placed one on top of each other and stacked up in the press. The press was a huge contraption in its own right, the top and the base each sculptured from whole tree trunks joined by two large threaded rods about 100m in diameter. It was operated by hand.

The farm labourers would turn down the compression wheels and when they could turn it no more, huge long poles, a bit like the ones used on a capstan on an old ship, were used to generate even more pressure to the cheese.

The result was apple juice, gallons of the stuff. The juice was transported and poured into large wooden barrels, some of which were in excess of 100-gallon capacity. Nothing else was added and a few months later the juice fermented into cider, some of which was consumed by the farm labourers, the surplus when possible was sold to generate farm income.

However, if you wanted to make cider you needed apples and if you wanted apples, you needed orchards and Dad had two fine orchards, one at the front of the house and one at the rear. These contained numerous varieties of apple as well as a few plum and pear trees thrown in.

Not all the apples were used for cider - there were eating apples and cooking apples, these were hand picked and stored in the old cheese room for home consumption during the winter, each of which had to be placed on old newspaper on the cheese room floor. A job for us kids under the supervision of our old spinster, Aunt Ivy, who insisted that a gap between each one was important so that if one went rotten, it would not contaminate its neighbour.

They were difficult to keep and many went bad long before Christmas. I always thought it was a bit of a waste of time, you spent hours placing them out and then you spent hours throwing them out. Brambly apples kept the best and made wonderful pies, and to this day Apple Pie, is still my favourite.

So, with the orchard also came wildlife in abundance, especially birds, sparrows, woodpeckers, the tit families, pigeons, rooks, crows, etc. I remember there where hundreds of birds flying, calling, singing, especially in the spring, all music to a young farm boy who was surrounded by nature at its best. The orchards also acted as wind breaks and was a godsend that protected us from the wind when it flew in from the north east. There is nothing as glorious as an orchard when it is in full blossom, except when its full of fruit!

One day I came home from school to a shocking sight. In the field where the orchard once stood was a large yellow bulldozer, parked up after a successful day and all the lovely trees lay on their sides with their roots exposed to the elements. I ran to the back of the house and to my delight that orchard was untouched and was a picture to my eyes after the devastation I had just witnessed.

But it was all short lived. When I came home next day that orchard had also been destroyed. The trees that once produced fruit would now only produce fire wood. It seemed such a shame. It took me a long time to get over the loss of the orchards. When the trees went so did the birds and the climbing frames that nature provide which we kids made good use of. It was now all lost. The wind blew in with a vengeance, we would now need all that firewood to keep warm. Paradise was lost and a long, farming tradition with it.

It was the new age, cider was not as popular with the new-age drinker, and it was being replaced with other sweet drinks as rationing on sugar products was being removed. Dad could not sell his cider and each year gallons had to be thrown away to make way for the new crop, but milk was in big demand so the fields that were once full of tree were now full of cows. I suppose it made sense at the time, but I'm glad that not all farmers had the same idea and the result is that we in North Wootton and surrounding parishes, can still enjoy the majesty of the humble Cider Apple Tree.

Lost but Not Forgotten.

A Passer By.

A BOY, A CART, A BOAT AND A CYCLE

A limited amount of old second-hand timber, two old axels with wheels, best located from an old pram and you had the ingredients to manufacture what we kids called a soap box cart or 'Dillies.'

The main chassis was a plank about 3-foot-long, to which the axels were attached. The rear axle fixed and the front one arranged so it could swivel on a centre pin, a short piece of rope attached to each side of the axel, enabled the cart to be steered from the single seat which was attached above the rear axle. We had great difficulty in keeping the axles affixed to the frame as bent over four inch nails were not the best engineering option for the job. This fault was rectified by Dad who supplied us with some nuts and bolts. The brakes were applied by sliding your feet against the surface over which you were travelling, simple but very effective.

Power was supplied by an older brother pushing from the back; accelerations depended on the strength and enthusiasm of the pusher.

Just up the road from the farm was a long hill, we called it Gould's Hill, as it approached our neighbours farm. After towing the cart to the top of the hill, it was turned to the downward direction, a nervous but exhilarated child was placed in the seat and then pushed vigorously towards its destiny, the cart gained its own velocity and carried away at great speed with its occupant screaming with fear and excitement. If all went well, and if a crash (which was often) was avoided, it could travel about half a mile to arrive back at the farm gate.

We gained no serious injuries from this exhilarating pastime, although we often ended up in the ditch, much to spectator's amusement, thank God there were not many cars on the roads in those days. I certainly would not condone this activity today but looking back I must say it was great fun.

Out in the field that was known as Spring Ground, arose an artesian well which supplied a small, but navigable pond, the water from which supplied the fresh water to the cow trough in the top cow yard. It was thought a good idea to create

Graham with his brothers, hard at work.

a small boat and navigate this small stretch of water, but of course to us kids it wasn't just a pond it was a raging sea just waiting to be tamed and explored.

The first obstacle to our navigational experience was the fact that we had no boat, quite a problem you might think, but not to us kids.

The attempt to remove Mother's old tin washing tub, was abandoned as it was affixed to a large nail driven into the high wall of Mum's wash house. The diligent search of the old farm buildings was rewarded by the discovery of half an old cider barrel that Dad had cut down to make into a water trough for the calves. The hole where the tap had been fitted was filled with a wooden plug from the wood store, and with a length of binder twine for the use of towing and navigation, we were in business.

The HMS Barrel, was duly towed, pushed, heaved and cursed, to the edge of the pond and launched successfully one sunny afternoon. One of us was placed in the barrel and launched into the centre of the pond and then carefully returned back to the side of the pond by slowly pulling the binder twine life line. It was great fun and we all had a great adventure a bit like Toad, Mole and Rat, but not quite.

One day our cousin visited and insisted that he should be allowed to partake in our great adventure. So, he was duly placed in the barrel and launched out with far too much exertion, the result was that the barrel slowly turned around several times and as a result the life line was slowly wrapping its self around the outside of the barrel. To rectify this, we pulled with even greater enthusiasm without thought of the consequences of our actions. The barrel span around at an alarming speed, our cousin instead of staying low in the craft decided to stand up, well you can imagine the result. Yes, he was catapulted out and landed in the water, much to his anger.

He was bigger and older than us and I remember that after he staggered from the edge of the pond, he chased us back to the sanctuary of the farm with gesticulations of catching and maiming us all.

Mother dried him out and calmed him down, tea was eaten and harmony was restored, and we all had a good laugh at his misfortune. However, Dad was not amused, he made us all aware of the dangers we had been in whilst playing on water and the HMS Barrel was returned to dry dock in the calf pen, never to be launched again.

Cycling was a must on our adventure's, punctures allowing, and we cycled miles. In fact from the age of 8 years old I had to cycle all the way to Coxley to attend school and later cycle home again, in all a journey of some 6 miles a day, 30 miles a week, seems a lot now but not at the time. Rain was not a deterrent as Mum bought me a huge yellow waterproof cape to wear, but your legs still got wet, and I spent many a school day sitting in the discomfort of wet trousers.

I must tell you a small story about the cousin who had the misfortune to fall from our makeshift boat. First, I must explain that the rear wheel of a bicycle contains a ratchet mechanism that allows you to stop pedalling and cruise along under the influence of momentum whilst your legs remained motionless.

My cousin had made up this cycle from spare parts as was the custom then, as new cycles were too expensive to purchase, well, the back wheel that he had fitted had what was called a fixed wheel, no ratchet installed. One day he accelerated away, showing off how fast his new construction was. The down side was that he had forgotten about the non-inclusion of a ratchet in the wheel, raised himself off the seat to tuck in his coat, the momentum of the power generated from the back wheel was transmitted to the pedals, and he was catapulted over the handle bars. It was funny but I must admit not for him, it took many days for his scraped knees to heal.

The fixed wheel ended up at the dump, and his Dad bought him a wheel with a ratchet firmly installed, but much to our jealousy it also contained a three-speed gearing mechanism that made his cycle far superior to ours, so I suppose he had the last laugh after all.

A time of, adventure, navigation, and learning curves.

A Passer By.

A BOY AND A SCHOOL

It was just another fantastic late summer day 1951, King George VI was still monarch, I was five years old enjoying the wonderful life of living on a Somerset dairy farm, not a care in the world. Another cherished day of playing with the farm dogs and running through the late summer grass and checking in the hedges to see if any birds where nesting late with their second batch of eggs.

Nature was thinking about changing the season from summer to the autumn but not yet, still many sunny days to come in the approaching Indian summer. September can be a wonderful month with lots of sunny days, trees to climb, hills to roll down country lanes to cycle and rivers to cross and navigate.

A time of great education for a small boy, shown by brothers and sisters, lessons taught to me by nature, such as never wear shoes when it should be welly boots, never leave home without a warm coat when the weather was unpredictable. Always tell someone where you are going in case your adventure turns into a misadventure. The countryside is full of adventure, nature is kind and generous, but she can also be cruel and destructive, but she should always be respected, loved, and cherished.

So, there I was living the life that every 5-year-old should, the love of a mother, the comfort of the farm house, with information and nature as my guide to the future. So, what else did I need? Well, I will tell you.

My mother mentioned something about school clothes and school shoes, but why to me? I knew that my siblings' school, was certainly not in my infant mind but yes, I was to start school the following week and no amount of protest was going to change my mother's determined intentions. My brothers assured me that I would be fine as they also attended the junior school and would keep an eye on me, well at least for the first day, after that it was up to me to make the effort.

As I stepped out of the comfort of the family car and said goodbye to my mum, I turned to see this large daunting Victorian building the internal workings of which were about to play a part in my future existence.

Graham and his trusty transport to school.

Coxley Junior School it was called and was approached from the road by a long open corridor. The school gable wall was prominent on one side, a high stone wall on the other and it led to the entrance of the boys' playground.

Situated to one side was a small stone built shed that would shelter the boys when sent out to play in wet weather, the girl's playground was next door separated from us by a high stone wall and contained a similar structure.

Having navigated the play areas, I entered into the domain of a Mrs McCormick, a teacher we would learn to love and respect.

The room was large with high ceilings, there were some radiators for warmth powered by a huge coal fired boiler situated in a shed next to the boys' toilet block. It was supplied with endless shovels of coal by a man dressed in an old Army Great Coat, but most of the heat came from a large Victorian coke-fired, cast iron stove that was situated in a prominent position within the compass of the room, surrounded by railings to stop the pupils from getting burnt. It was very efficient and I always envied those children whose desk was located in its proximity.

I guess the winters in those days were colder than now, as many days milk that was provided in one third pint bottles for all children and delivered by the local dairy, was frozen on delivery and the stove was very efficient at thawing it out.

Mrs McCormick was the only teacher in that junior class of about 30 pupils. It was a mixed class, there were 3 separate rooms in the school with total population of about 60 children, from the age of 5 years to 11 years.

Lots of the children like me were from agricultural backgrounds, and we all got on well from the start and now 71 years later I am still friends with many of them.

At the start of school, we were not supplied with books or paper to write on, instead we were given a piece of slate bound inside a wooden frame. We used white chalk to record the information being installed in us by our inspiring teacher and after the lesson was concluded we had to wipe the slate clean with a damp cloth that was sent around the room, so as you can see no information was recorded, only what you could retain in your head, in my case not for long.
At this tender age we were taught how to sew with needle and thread, also how to knit and I remember knitting a scarf, it was about one inch (30mm) wide and 6 inches (150mm long.)
Art was encouraged, and by now we had paper to draw on, the one large easel situated at the front of the class on which I never got to draw or paint was always used by one girl who was obviously a teacher's pet.

Situated geographically next to the school was Coxley Church with its large burial ground. One day the class was disrupted by the sound of the church bell, its single toll would repeat itself about every minute and its echo bounced around the room. This of course sent us naïve children into a fit of giggles only to be reprimanded by the teacher who tried to explain that a funeral was about to take place and we should all show a quiet respect. Some of us were only five years of age and understood little of what was being explained.

Graham and his brother
Peter sat on the school wall

School meals were always good although I never got used to the taste of figs, which often found their way onto the menu, or the potatoes that always had large black spots in them even when they were mashed.

The Christmas menu was always a real treat which we looked forward to each year, with cakes and chocolate biscuits, a rare treat indeed during the years of rationing that was introduced during the Second World War and was still in place.

These meals had to be paid for. My mother would give me the money to give to the teacher who would record it in a large ledger and if there was change. One day I had a Farthing in change so I went to the shop to buy a tea cake, unfortunately the cake was valued at a half- penny, so the lady in the shop cut the tea cake in half and sold me the other half, I wonder if that would happen today? For your information, in those days there were 960 farthings in a Pound Sterling.

During those early years the basics of learning was slowly making an impression on my young mind and to be able to read and write through the vehicle of education would prove to be a major advantage for my future. I always had a problem with spelling, although I did develop superb hand writing and to this day I prefer to use a fountain pen.

Mathematics was my favourite and the Times Table was a must, not sure if they teach it today what with the introduction of computers and calculators. I've always believed if the advancing technology moves beyond the bounds of human understanding then we will all become idiots.

At the age of about 7 years I was promoted to the middle class, the domain of a male teacher. I won't mention his name as I disliked him a lot. He behaved harshly and handed out discipline with an old slipper. I tell you now, if a pupil hates his tutor, the former will learn nothing from the latter.

It was in this class that I was promoted to Ink Monitor, I need to explain that the only pens available were Ink pens, which consisted of a steel nib attached to a small thin wooden handle, the nib was dipped before use into the Ink wells that are an integral part of the school desk. It was my job to make sure all Ink wells were kept full, doesn't sound much but it was a respected, important responsibility.

At this time, Carbide was used to fuel bicycle lamps.

Carbide mixed with water produced Acetylene, a very combustible gas. Well one day a disruptive pupil brought some carbide to school and proceeded to place some in the Ink wells, well this caused the ink to fizz and bubble out of its container and run all down the top of the desks, much to everyone's amusement, this chemical reaction would only end when the small particle had fully dissolved. I can tell you those ink stains remained on those desks and were still there years later when I left that school.

I remember one day the room was evacuated as a horrible smell was detected, however with prompt efficiency the culprit, a dead rat, was removed from below the wooden floor by a Council Official and normality was restored.

The floors were constructed from heavy sawn Elm boards and as most of the boys wore hobnailed boots you can imagine the noise created when the children ran toward the playground at break time.

Playtime was enjoyed by all, a time to dispose of all that pent-up emotion and energy, this was achieved through lots of skipping with a long rope and two energetic operatives, up to six kids could skip simultaneously, changing personnel, as one ran out another would run in and take their place. Also bean bag throwing was a popular pastime and playing Conkers when in the season.

Keep fit classes were always encouraged, they were also compulsory. There was a large playing field adjacent to the school and enjoy numerous activities, especially P.T and sport.

Two years later through a natural process of progression I was moved to the senior class under the direction of the head mistress Miss Blackwell. It was at this time that my mother decided I was old enough to cycle to school, so from that day forwards in all weather, I cycled to and from school, a cumulative of 6 miles a day.

It was Miss Blackwell's job to finely tune our junior education and prepare us for the next big hurdle – the senior school at Wells. She was an excellent, although strict teacher and administered her class with profound fairness. She won our respect and we gave her the attention she deserved.

One day she was sitting on her high Dias in a very quiet mood, not like her at all. She became very pale and one of the girls went to seek the attention of another teacher. It was discovered that she was suffering from a broken arm from an accident at home but that was not going to prevent her from attending to our education.

During this time the Council had commissioned a new school room to be constructed in part of the playing field and the older pupils were encourage to get involved. Activities included studying copies of the construction plans and regular visits to the site, even to discuss construction methods with the building operatives.

After this brief encounter with a subject outside the vocation of farming, I had a strong feeling that later in my life, construction would play a big part of my destiny, after all, my grandfather and my great uncles on my mother's side were Master Builders. My grandfather died when I was very young but it was obvious to me that I had inherited the genes.

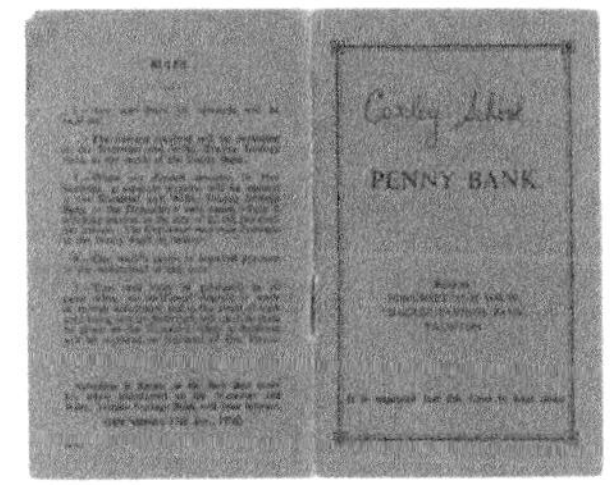

Then there was the arrival at school of a number of Hungarian refugees, whom we were pleased to accept into the class and to assist in their ability to learn the English language and the culture of English society.

It was in this class that we were taught basket making, also book making, learning how to sew the pages into a book which we were proud to take home. We even made papier Mache puppet heads from wet soaked newspaper around plasticine moulds and on completions the heads were painted in bright colours.

You will have noticed in this article, those arts and crafts were my favourite subjects, the dexterity of my hands being used actively as a superior tool in my journey through my education.

There were two schools in Wells, the Blue Grammar if you managed to pass the eleven plus exam, or be thrown to the wolves, at what was then called the Secondary School. Thankfully for me my father sent me to a fine school professed to be for the education of young gentlemen.

And may he always be blessed for that wise decision.

A time to learn, time to play, & time to respect discipline.

A Passer By.

A BOY AND A PIG

I have always considered it a privilege to have been born on a Somerset dairy farm along with my two sisters and two brothers. I was the youngest, born in 1946, a place where I continued to live and farm for the following 49 years.

It was not always an easy life as we kids were expected to do all sorts of chores around the farm especially on Saturdays and Sundays when the farm employees had time off, it was hard work but it had its rewards and supplied many tales to tell.

My father kept a large sow, I can't remember the breed, I think it was a Large White, or a Landrace? This large pig was housed in rather luxurious conditions in a purpose made shelter on a strip of land by the top of the farm kitchen garden. I think Dad was rather proud of her and he used to show her off to his cousins in Dulcote where he would take her to visit the boar pig which my uncles owned. She had an enjoyable existence, well fed from all the waste food from the farm house mixed with grain meal to produce a feed we called swill. It was all subsidised with high protein pig nuts, which arrived via Sheldon's in large one hundred weight hessian bags. I couldn't lift these large bags as I was only about 12 years old at the time so used to transfer the nuts into a small bucket and take it to her a bucket at a time. She had her own make shift swimming pool, for on the hot summer days she would walk round to the cattle trough in the home paddock and sit in the cooling waters. She could wander wherever the desire took her as she had free range of the whole 200 acre farm.

She produced many litters of pigs in return for the luxuries bestowed on her, some of the piglets ended up as prime fat bacon pigs in Grandad's lead salter, to be cured as salt pigs and bacon for home consumption; the surplus pigs were reared for bacon and taken to Shepton, or Farrington Gurney Markets for sale by auction.

In one litter there was a runt being the smallest and unhealthiest member of the babies. Father was reluctant to dispose of this small runt, so I was dispatched each morning to take extra warm cows' milk to this individual which it disposed of with relish. If I was late taking the milk it would come looking for it, sometimes right up to the farmhouse door where it would wait patiently to be fed. Afterwards it would run back to the safety of its mother and siblings. Pigs are more intelligent than some people credit them.

Later that summer when the oak trees were dropping their acorns, (now pigs just love acorns), our pig was thought to have gone on a great adventure.

Father received a phone call from our farming neighbour who farmed at Launcherley, which is about a mile away as the crow flies, to say that our pig was in his home field under the oak tree eating the acorns, that he thought should be reserved for his own pig.

Father was very apologetic as it doesn't pay to fall out with your neighbour, especially a farming neighbour. Father was cursing to himself for allowing his pig to have liberty to free range over such a large area and also the pig for taking advantage of his generosity.

He despatched me immediately to collect the pig and return it to its drastically reduced liberty zone.

I was armed with a short stick in one hand with which to protect myself from being eaten by this now large beast, also I could use it to persuade her to move forwards. I used a short piece of tin sheet in the other to steer her, for if

you place the tin sheet against her right eye she will turn to the left and likewise if you present the tin to her left eye, she will turn right, well that's the theory anyway.

So, I arrived in my neighbour's field, armed and thankfully our neighbour was nowhere to be seen as I had been expecting to get a rollicking from him for bad pig husbandry and allowing her to roam so far from our farm.

My first attempts to move her proved impossible. She was determined not to be evacuated from such a prime source of her favourite food until such time as she had her fill. She was large and I was small so there was no competition as to who was in charge of whom.

I eventually managed to move her towards our destination a

mile away, several times she turned on me, pushed past and ran with unbelievable speed back to the oak tree, to continue her banquet and I had to start out all over again.

It was on one of the hardest tasks so far in my life at the age of 12 years but there was no way I was going to be defeated in this responsibility my father had laid at my door, after all, he was trusting me to return his pride and joy the pig that is, not me!

I wonder sometimes if kids nowadays at the age of twelve would take on such a task and also if parents today would find it irresponsible to despatch such a young child to collect such a large animal, especially one that could be potentially lethal. The days of ships made of wood and men made of steel and all that, I suppose, comes to mind.

Eventually after sweat and tears, and I don't mind admitting that during that journey I was reduced to tears of frustration: why did our pig not want come home, what was wrong with her?

Well, the triumph and glory was mine. I had eventually coaxed, threatened and driven that selfish sow back to her home next to that plot of land, next to the kitchen garden. With pride of a job well done and a chest puffed out to prove it, I informed Dad, that his pig was home. I think he was proud of me, I like to think so, but unfortunately, he rarely gave out praise to anyone except maybe Winston Churchill. When Dad opened up the pig shelter to put the pig in, he stopped short. There was my pig in the shelter!

The neighbour then phoned to ask if we had seen his pig! Before he phoned the first time why did our neighbour not check that it was his pig that was under his oak tree, and not ours and why didn't Dad or me, check to see if our pig was in fact missing, before I embarked on this episode of a complete waste of a good day and my energy.

Happy Days.

A Passer By.

A BOY AND A STORM

I was 16 years old and it was Boxing Day night, the wind blew in from the east with a vengeance and with a message that the mild winter so far, was over.

I was on my way to one of the farm labourer's cottage with Dad, Mum and my brothers for an evening of festivities. On leaving the cottage later that night it began to snow. I noticed that the snow was different to the snow I had seen before; this was not wet snow with large flakes but dry and blew in the wind not unlike icing sugar or fine grains of sand.

Arriving back at the farmhouse and warmed up by sitting by the AGA stove we went in search of the comfort of hot water bottles and bed only to be woken several times in the night by the howl of the wind through the old attic timbers and an old piece of loose galvanised sheeting rattling away somewhere outside.

Next morning, Dad had us all up early with the news that he could not start milking as the snow was blocking the door to the milking parlour and some of the yard gates were buried under large drifts, these had to be cleared away before milking could commence.

The cows were all tied up inside by neck chains in what we called the long stall so each morning you had to release them. On this occasion I noticed that everything inside the stall was covered in snow to an average depth of about 3 inches (75mm). The hay, the bedding straw and even on the cows backs. This was because the stall was roofed in clay pan tiles, these where ill-fitting and the snow had blown though the gaps in the tiles, there was no felt membrane under the tiles like there is today.

The light of day told the true story, all the roads leading to the farm were blocked level with the top of the hedges, this meant the milk lorry could not collect the supply of milk. Desperate action had to be taken. Dad tied a large tow chain to his little Morris 1000 pickup truck, hooked up his largest tractor and took off across the fields, about a mile to the nearest village situated on a main road.

At Dulcote the truck was left at my uncle's farm, there to stay for 8 weeks, the road to Wells was soon made passable by a large loading shovel hired in by the County Council from the local quarries to clear local main roads but the

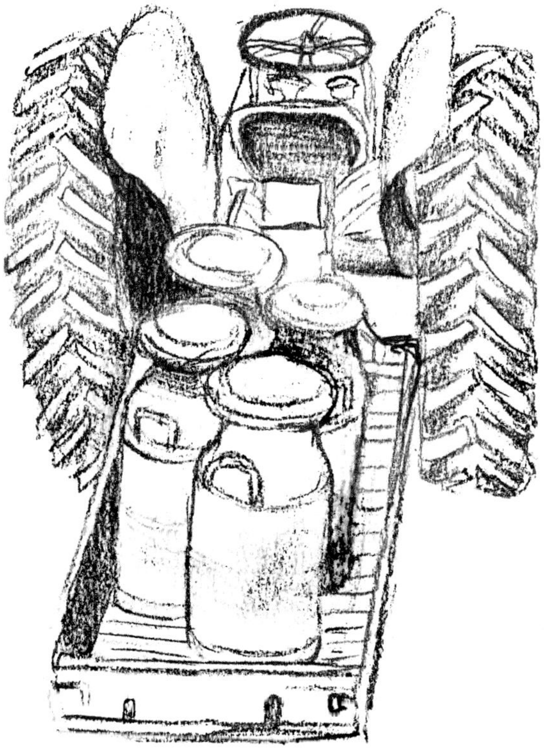

side lanes stayed blocked. The council concentrated their efforts on important communication routes, therefore all local village lanes had to wait their turn.

So, every day Dad transported the milk by tractor and link box to Dulcote, loaded it into the truck and took it into Wells where Mr Ruff was waiting to bottle it for his milk round and return with the empty churns ready for the next day's consignment.

Once a week Mother would take her large winter coat and scarf and join the milk run to collect supplies that were needed to see us through another week. You have to remember that tractors did not have tractor cabs. One of the most important supplies was the paraffin and wicks for the oil stove used to help heat the house. This was purchased from Whiting of Wells who still trade in Wells from the original site.

The day after the original storm that caused all the inconvenience, started the big freeze. If I remember rightly, it

The top yard at Wellesley Farm.

stayed below freezing night and day for nearly 6 weeks. Everything froze even the diesel in the tractors, we had to wrap the tractor fuel tank and filters with Hessian sacks to keep them going for a little while. Dad left one tractor running night and day to guarantee he had at least one to use.

All the water supplies froze, we were lucky in the fact that we had a supply of water from a spring which flowed underground to an old stone water trough in the main cow yard. This was thanks to the Victorian farmers who created this invaluable supply and this ran all the time despite how cold it got. We just broke the ice in the trough each morning.

Lots of tales, not enough space.

The snow blocked the lane to the farm on 26th December 1962 and was cleared by Burt Coombes who still lives in the village, driving a Fowler single cylinder Bulldozer in the third week of February 1963.

Lots of our readers will have experience of the winter of 63 and all have tales to share, I'm just sharing a few of mine.

Cold Times.

A Passer By.

A BOY AND UNUSUAL ANIMALS

If you remember, I told you about father's prize pig that he thought had gone on walkabout to look for acorns. Well, he had another pig before that, she was kept for breeding in a galvanized pig pen, out next to the orchard hedge in the home paddock, and she also had the run of the field.

Old Albert Diment who looked after Dad's pigs apart from other farm duties, went to clean out her sty one day and found her dead just outside the door of the sty. Dad called the vet to carry out a post-mortem to identify this sudden and unexpected death.

The diagnosis was Anthrax; now this was a serious and notifiable disease and the vet explained that the Ministry of Agriculture and the local police had to be informed immediately.

Within a short time, the Ministry vet had arrived and confirmed the cause of death, he rang the police station and the local police officer from Coxley arrived on his bicycle to take charge of and oversee the operations that had to take place.

First, Dad had to stop all other work on the farm as all hands where needed to dig a large pit all by hand as no JCB's were available in those days. Next, the pit was lined with a thick layer of straw then a layer of wood and then a layer of coal from Dad's boiler store, when the pyre was completed to the ministry manual and to the policeman's satisfaction, the pig was laid thereon and the pyre was lit.

We kids were allowed to watch all that was going on (I was about six years old at the time), as long as we did not get too close to the infected pig. We did not need any counselling afterwards as farm kids were used to dead animals, it came with the territory, and we certainly did not lose any sleep over what we had witnessed.

My uncle Ralph Thorner had a slaughter house at Pylle on

the Fosse, and when Dad and Mum went to visit, we kids used to be shown all that was going on in the slaughter house by our cousins. Once, my uncle blew up a pig's bladder with air so we could use it as a football, just imagine anyone doing that today, he would probably get arrested for traumatizing young children.

Anyway. back to my story. The pig was burnt and the ashes were buried in the pyre pit, all infections destroyed and life at the farm returned to normal. Apparently, anthrax spores can lay dormant in the soil for many years only rarely infecting any unsuspecting animals rooting around in the soil. Louis Pasteur developed a vaccine in 1881 for animals and a vaccine was available for humans in 1955.

Down in the old tin workshop lived an old red hen, not sure why but I think it escaped when father sold his old laying stock to a company in Weston-Super-Mare who were in the poultry processing business. Their name was Wells, and the family owned the Webbington Country Club and as Dad disposed of his old hens and through them, he and others became Life Members. This entitled them to free access to the club which in those days had a casino. Apparently in those days you were not allowed in unless you wore black tie. However, I digress.

Anyway, this old hen had an unusual habit, as a result of which we kids called her the Indian Hen. Amongst all the old nuts, bolts and spanners that were untidily strewn across the work bench was a half empty cardboard box of galvanised roofing nails, they were about 3 Inches long (75mm) very sharp, with large heads. Every day at about 12 noon this old hen would wander through after being out foraging, hop into the box of nails, shuffle round until she was comfortable and lay her egg.

We all thought this most amusing as she had plenty of soft warm places to lay, but no, she decided the nails where best. Dad used to say 'typical female', but at that tender age I did not understand what he meant. I cannot remember what happened to the Indian Hen; I like to think she lived to great age, but more likely ended up as a fox banquet, as did most free-range hens.

I told you once about how it was part of our duties as kids to assist on the farm and one of these duties was with the rearing of the young calves. Feeding and bedding them down were the usual chores, so we got to know these lovely animals and I can see them now, all lined up waiting for their rations of milk, eyes full of trust as we had become their surrogate mums.

We had to teach them how to drink from a bucket, as it was natural only to suck their mothers' teats. This was achieved by getting the calf to suck your milky fingers and slowly lowering your hand into the milk in the bucket, they soon got the hang of this within a few feeds.

There was one calf I remember most of all and we called him Burt, not sure why but we soon realised that Burt was what you might call, not the sharpest tool in the tool box, in fact he was as daft as a brush. He always wanted to be with humans rather than be with his cohorts, he was the favourite animal in the eyes of the farm labourers.

He lived on the farm for many years as even Dad did not want to send him to Market as it would upset so many on the farm, so Burt lived a charmed life. But like so many things on a farm, one day Burt was missing and Dad never admitted what really became of him. I like to think he went to live in a park but he probably ended up at Uncle Ralph Thorners.

We had many dogs on the farm, working dogs, so not really house pets but even so, they were very affectionate, and we kids loved them.

One day one of the dogs ran in front of the grass mower and lost one of its back legs. We all thought that Dad would have her put down but no, Dad loved his dogs so he spent a small fortune with the vet to save her. It was all a great success, and within days the dog was running around on three legs with great dexterity.

She continued her farm duties, collecting the cows at milking times and moving stock around the farm fields, she also used to round up the hens, although I don't think she was supposed to do that. We also had a dog that liked to bite car tyres, but that's another story.

Unusual Days.

A Passer By.

A BOY AND LOCAL PASTIMES

When we were kids swimming was a great summer pastime, and to full-fill our desires we had to go to the local swimming pool in Wells. The baths where located next to the old fire station opposite the old cattle market. The site of the old pool is now better known as the Tesco Store Site and car park, the only screaming sounds now coming from the site are car tyres, where once it was the shrill cry of excited girls as we chased them around the pool.

It was quite a large outdoor pool and it boasted three diving boards, a high board, a middle board, and a spring board. Years later a lot of pools demolished their high diving boards only leaving the spring boards, as they were described by so called experts, as dangerous to the public swimming under them. There may be some truth in this, but what happened to common sense, if there is someone diving then keep away from that area, or vice versa. The fact that no one was ever dived onto the whole time I was at the pool, didn't come into the equation, bureaucracy is a wonderful thing, if the majority are enjoying themselves, the minority are always trying to stop it happening.

Many years later when I was in to contracting, I was asked by a local builder to weld up the broken brackets on the spring board, this was accomplished, and I was invited by the builder to test my work by testing the boards stability. As I ventured out to the end, I was almost pitched into the water but saved by the quick actions of the builder who grabbed hold of the anchor points to stop it flying up in the air. Apparently he forgot to put in the retaining pins, not sure if that was correct but an accident with a diving board was avoided, and we had a good laugh afterwards.

Wells pool was about two miles away from the Farm as the crow flies, and to get there we had to walk, so loaded up with swimming trunks and towels we set off down the farm lane, picked up the foot path that led down gypsy lane across the Forty Acre field to arrive at the railway line. This was still very much in use at that time, so caution had to be observed before a crossing was attempted; first was to listen out for the sound of a train, if it was travelling towards Shepton Mallet it would be very loud puffing under its heavy load usually strawberries from the Cheddar valley (yes, they were still steam trains). If they were running under momentum down the slope from Shepton Mallet you had difficulty in hearing them, but having made this journey many times, my elder brothers were experienced and always got us younger ones across safely.

Sometimes we would leave a half penny coin on the line with the anticipation that if the train rolled over it while we were away it would be transformed into a penny piece, however this experiment always failed, but it was fun to see how the heavy vehicle had converted the coin into a thin roll of copper strip. Following the foot path, it took us past the Engineering works (now Morrisons), we arrived in Silver street, then it was only a short walk to the pool.

We could only use the pool during the summer months as it was an outdoor pool, there were no indoor pools, so during the closed season we found other things to do.

The railway line that we had to cross to get to Wells, ran up to Shepton Mallet and beyond, in doing so traversed along the edge of the majestic Dulcote Hill, and it was this line that navigated us to our next adventure.

When we were kids Dulcote Hill was still a fine hill, there was a small active quarry, owned by Foster Yeoman near the Wells side, and an old disused Quarry that was once operated by The Great Western Rail Company around about 1885 to extract ballast for its western extension and maintenance.

It was this old disused quarry that acted like a magnet to us kids, also to our cousins and our mates from the village. To gain access to the site we again had to navigate the railway line, a very dangerous exercise as part of the section was in a narrow cutting, and if our parents knew what we were doing, there would have been hell to pay.

We were adventurous kids but were wise to the dangers that surrounded us, and common sense and precautions kept us out of danger.

On entering the site of the old disused quarry, we were met with a glorious site that only Mother Nature could supply.

There was no machinery left on the site but you could make out the old foundations of once occupied buildings, there was one small stone building intact, hidden in the trees on the far side of the quarry complete with a heavy door onto which was attached a sign that read "Danger Explosives". Of course, we had to venture in and as I'm here to tell the tale it contained only spiders hiding in the dark corners.

We also discovered a Well which was stone lined and very deep. We used to drop stones down it, count the seconds until they hit the water and try and estimate how deep it was. The only covering it had was an old sheet of rusty corrugated roofing tin, it was very dangerous so we avoided that part of the site thereafter.

Nature had transformed the site to a glorious vision to youngsters eyes, small tree saplings of all varieties grew out of old scalping spoil heaps and the old rail and horse tracks were now covered in a type of alpine vegetation.

In the summer months we used to pick wild strawberry's which grew in abundance. It was a discontinued industrial site but nature had taken it back as its own and its magnificence was all around us. Long lengths of small link chains still hung from the rock face, as a testament to the quarry men who were probably supported by them as they prised the rock from the face.

We also discovered an old disused firing range with a butt constructed from sandbags from which we prised used disfigured bullet heads, these we treasured as valuable finds, also lots of discarded used rifle and pistol shells lay abandoned at various distances from the Butts. This site was probably used by the home guard, or other military organisation, for shooting practice during the previous years of world conflict.

It was probably not the safest of playgrounds, but we came to no harm and the experienced we gained could never have been learnt in a schoolroom. To us kids' life was one great adventure and the ability to stay safe and healthy in these environments could only come from education and first hand experience.

I wonder if kids get the same satisfaction from life today, with their heads buried in some electronic game, or walking around with ear plugs listening to meaningless rubbish or texting their friends instead of meeting up with them and having lots of adventures as we did.

My advice to kids today; the world is full of adventure and fun, don't sit alone and get depressed, get together with your mates, go out discover it and enjoy it.

Years later the site was taken over by the council who used it as a refuge site, over the years it was filled, covered in soil and reinstated with a plantation of trees. All very nice and tidy but I wish it had been left as a heritage site and nature reserve for all to enjoy.

It was there but now it's gone.

A Passer By.

A BOY AND HIS RATIONS

Today when we visit the shops and super stores food and commodities of every description are there in abundance although albeit sourced from all over the world, not so much home produced any more.

I guess Frank Whittle had a lot to do with that, his jet engine which I'm sure has since been vastly improved and with the addition of plentiful supplies of aviation fuel, has made all this possible.

In all my life I have never seen food and clothes so cheaply to buy as they are today, something, I'm told is to do with sweat shops in foreign lands and something to do with the difference in the economies of countries of production and countries of distribution.

Whatever the reason, it appears that we are all over supplied and spoilt for choice, so much so that the stocks of charity shops are overwhelmed with goods, which leave their doors even cheaper.

I once remember years ago, a politician whose name escapes me, stood up in Parliament and stated that "We have never had it so good," well maybe the words of that politician have finally come true.

There was also a politician who once said in the early days of electrical power that electric would be so cheap to purchase, that only the rich would be able to afford candles, well I don't think that ever came true, do you!

I was born in 1946 and the effect of World War Two meant that the supply of every commodity available to the public was very limited. I was about 5 years old when I remember Mum taking me on a shopping trip to Bristol and I remember asking her why did people have wallpaper on the outside of their houses? She explained to me that what I was looking at was in fact the inside of people's houses or what was left of them.

I was too young to understand about German bombs and air raids, and it was very strange to see a house intact and then heaps of rubble for about 100 yards, then more houses intact. These houses had probably been bombed in the early part of the war so the damage I witnessed was several years old and some sites had small tree saplings growing through the rubble, along with brambles and bushes. It is amazing how Nature soon took it all back. These sites were repeated all over Bristol and when we finally parked the car it was on a car park constructed from materials from bomb sites or constructed on a bomb site. I think National Car Parks surveyed and constructed these, but I may well be wrong. However back to my story.

Mum had this little book which was issued by the Government and inside were little stamps, a very important book as without it you could not legally purchase certain commodities. These stamps were called ration stamps or coupons, you were only allowed so many, and if you used up your ration, then you could not get any additional food until the Government department issued you with your next allocation.

This of course led to what was called the Black Market of goods, these where items obtained by dealers from dubious source and sold on the open market with secrecy without the need for ration coupons. If a dealer was caught in this profession, it usually ended up with a custodial sentence at His Majesty's Pleasure.

Graham with his mother (Molly) and brothers Richard and Peter.

Living on a Farm at this time had great advantages as there was no shortage of dairy products, butter was made on the farm along with cheese, the hens supplied eggs and every farmer worth his salt reared a pig for home consumption.

Uncle Ralph, who I told you before owned a slaughter house, would arrive at the farm, and he would dispatch the pig, butcher it into joints and Grandad would salt it down. All legal as long as it was for home consumption, we were not allowed to market it.

When Dad was a young boy, he went to work for a while on a farm in America, this was before the outbreak of the 2nd World War and he became great friends with this farming family and during this time of food rationing in the UK, they would send over food parcels at regular intervals. These contained a wondrous amount of goods that were unattainable in England, especially I remember it contained sweets and canned peaches, sugar and all sorts of treats that Mum needed but were unavailable in the local shops.

My elder brother took a can of peaches and hid it and about 20 years later it was found when an electrician took up a loose floor board in the old cheese room much to everybody' s amusement.

We were indeed indebted to the Pearce Family for all that they did for us and Mr & Mrs Pearce came to England on a visit. I think it was about 1956 but not sure, certainly before the peaches gave up their hiding place.

We played football a lot on the front lawn. The farm house had these nice large sliding windows and of course on occasion a badly directed ball would cause considerable damage. Dad had to get a carpenter out from Wells to place plywood where the glass had been until glass was made available which took many weeks.

Finally, in time, as the countries of the world got back working together, rationing was removed from all goods but certainly the shortages taught us youngsters to appreciate things and look after them.

No throwaway society then and do you know what, it wouldn't do the youngster of today any harm to experience shortages and stop moaning over nothing.

Bad Times to Good Times.

A Passer By.

A BOY AND HIS GRANDFATHER

My Grandfather was what you might call a gentleman farmer. I never saw him shabbily dressed and he always wore a suit with his watch and chain secured to his waistcoat. He stood with a military stance which I guess came from his military training during the Anglo Boar War in South Africa. According to his medal he was there in 1901 and 1902 in which year the war ended.

He was a volunteer in the North Somerset Imperial Yeomanry and as far as we are aware he had to take his own horse. The Boars that the British army were engaged in were what you might call a guerrilla force, mostly drawn from South African farmers and landowners of which were mostly of Dutch descent. They were very mobile on their sturdy ponies and they ran rings around the British infantry, so a yeomanry regiment was required to match then in fighting ability and mobility.

It was a voluntary regiment, made up of farmers and country landowners. The requirements were you had to be competent at riding a horse and be a good shot with a gun; it was farmers sent to kill other farmers, not that nice when you think of it but that was the War Department Intentions.

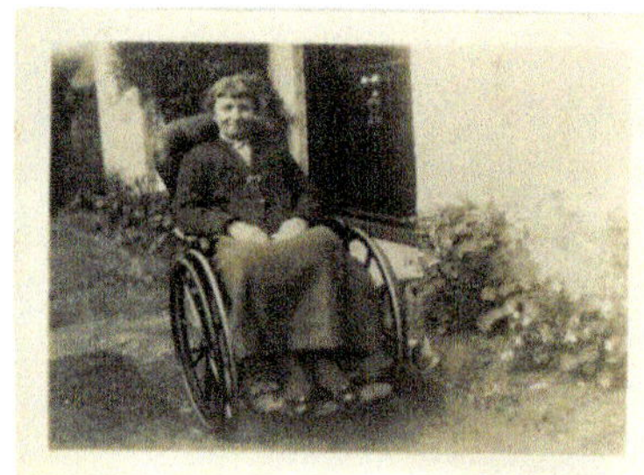

Graham's Grandmother Lillian Kate Watts at Wellesley Farm.

My Grandmother was of a sickly nature and suffered very badly with Rheumatoid Arthritis. I remember her either in her wheelchair or mostly in bed, unable or too painful to get up, she was confined to her bed for most of her later years.

Unfortunately, she died when I was about 4 years old so I never really got to know her, but I still have the vision of her sat in bed and wiping her eyes with a hanky, with the aid of a short tee shaped hazel nut stick which Grandfather had made for her, it was a useful aid because of her infirmity she had reduced use of her arms.

My Grandfather had retired to a house in Shepton Mallet opposite where the Tadley Acre estate is today. My spinster

Graham's Grandfather Sydney Austin Watts preparing for the Boer war.

aunt lived with them as a carer, she told me once how she took a full reel of cotton thread, placed it in an empty biscuit tin and when my Grandmother was asleep placed it under her bed. The end of the thread was laid under the door and up the stairs to my aunt's bedroom.

My Grandmother slept downstairs so as my aunt pulled the end of the thread the reel ran around in the tin - apparently it took my Grandfather some time to find the source of this annoying noise, much to my aunts amusement.

One of my aunts duties was to clean the house and I remember she used a goose wing complete with feathers as a duster, it was very efficient and she would wash it when soiled. Cooking was done on a gas cooker in a back room of the house; I will always remember that funny smell of gas that seemed to get into every part of the house.

When Mum and Dad went out to a function or a dance we were dispatched to stay with Grandfather and this was always a great adventure. We slept in the front bedroom, all three of us in a large feather bed and we listened to the traffic as it passed the house, a new experience for three boys brought up on a farm, miles from a main road.

My aunt would get two kitchen chairs, place a piece of timber between them and construct this very narrow but substantial bed. She slept in the same room to care for us and I guess we occupied her usual bed and I'm sure her temporary bed could not have been comfortable.

My Grandfather had this large cockerel that lived with the hens that provided eggs for the house, he gave us his walking stick and he instructed us how to approach the bird which always lowered its head when approached. He said: "Now just tap that stick on the ground in front of his beak." We did this and of course it would chase us around the field much to Grandfather's amusement. Now I know where my aunt got her sense of humour and I think I might be tarred with the same brush!!

Outside the house was an area paved with large blue lias stone slabs, Grandfather gave us paint brushes and instructed us to paint all the slabs. He supplied us with tins of water instead of paint, this was great fun, but if it was a hot day we never seemed to finish the job as the first slabs painted had dried out long before we could complete our task. What did I say about his sense of humour? Thinking back, we were a bit gullible but it kept us amused for hours.

Winter time was best, Shepton Mallet was about 600ft higher than our farm so when we had rain often Shepton had snow. Grandfather's field, was surrounded by a high dry stone wall and this resulted in large snow drifts building up on the sheltered side of the wall. We would spend hours digging out Igloos in the drifts to play in, and afterwards it was back to the house to warm our toes on the coal fire and enjoy large mugs of hot Ovaltine, it was fun drinking it through long glass straws which I think were used by Grandmother as a drinking aide when she was alive.

Grandfather taught me lots of crafts, from how to make a whistle out of a nut hazel branch, timber mole-traps, spars that were used to keep thatch secure, to repairing a puncture in a bicycle tyre, sharpen a pen knife, plus many more crafts that put me in fine stead for a life lived in the countryside.

If I can get my own Grandsons off their iPads, who knows, perhaps, I will be able to pass on my skills and experience to them. My own Grandfather passed away when I was just 14 years old, I wish he had lived longer as I could have learnt so much more from him, but he was 84 years old and suffered no serious illness. Just imagine he was 70 years old when I was born and I was the youngest of his 16 Grandchildren, to me he was a legend.

Young and Old together.

A Passer By.

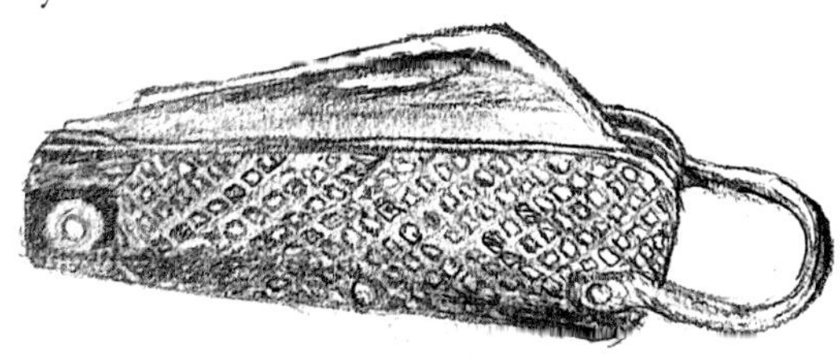

A BOY AND THE DEALER

We were on our way to Wells on the Glastonbury approach road and Mum pulled the car up to an abrupt stop, on looking out of the window for the reason I saw that the railway gates were across the road and securely closed. We were parked outside what is now the Tincknell agricultural store and the new roundabout on the Wells relief road.

The gates were closed because the train was about to cross the road, either going up towards Shepton Mallet or going down towards Weston-Super-Mare or even Burnham or Glastonbury.

There was a signal box next to the line and the train driver who, if travelling towards Shepton Mallet had to hand over the one and only key that would allow the train to travel over the section of line from Weston to Wells. He would hand it to the signalman or Station Master and collect the key for the section of line that allowed the train to enter that section of track leading to Shepton Mallett and beyond.

This Track Key system was used as it was a single track line and was designed and adopted by the Victorian railway companies, successfully to avoid head on crashes. There was only one key and I think it had to be inserted into a machine at the signal box to allow the signal to open the upward line and close the signal on the downward but I'm not absolutely sure of that fact.

When I was a child, the railway was still the greatest mode of transport and all manner of goods were transported efficiently all over the country. I remember on one occasion having to go with Dad to collect day old baby chicks that had arrived at the Somerset and Dorset station which was sited where today Halfords have their outlet store. Also riding into Wells with the tractor driver to collect wet sugar beet which had to be unloaded by hand from large railway trucks located in the station yard operated by The Great Western Railway Company, the site now occupied by Travis Perkins and Lidl.

Daily there were passengers travelling to work or on vacation, kids travelling to and back from school and sometimes cattle dealers travelling to the local markets. One of these dealers told me one day how he would buy ducks at the local market, get on a train and sit picking the feathers from the carcases

as he travelled towards London, where on arrival he would sell them to a poultry dealer before setting off to buy horses.

He explained to me that because the horses employed in London in those early days had to pull heavy carts over cobbled street the poor animals' careers where rather short due to leg and hoof problems, but he knew that if he brought these same animals back to Somerset and they were employed to pull agricultural machinery on soft fields their life expectancy was greatly increased. He bought them cheap from the streets of London, brought them home on the train knowing he would make a handsome profit.

This trade would continue until the lorry replaced the horses in London and the agricultural tractor replaced the carthorse in the field.

Another dealer told me that one day his son was old enough and trusted to go to the local market on his own to buy calves for rearing or slaughter, but all the older experienced dealers gave him a hard time and did not allow him to purchase a single animal to take back to his father.

On returning home the story was told and the father said: "Don't worry about it son, next week I will come with you." On that day the said dealer bought every calf that was for sale regardless of the cost. He then turned to the other dealers and said: "This is my son don't you ever treat him like that again," and he stormed out of the auction house. The son continued and he was in the dealing business for many years and was given the respect that he deserved.

It has to be remembered that in those days, most towns had cattle markets and the farmers brought their animals to these convenient locations to trade with and the dealers, butchers and other farmers looking for stock replacements.

Wells had a large and respected cattle market, it was situated where the Bus Station now operates. I was informed from a reliable source that during the war years some of the cattle dealers got involved in the Black Market, which supplied goods to customers outside of the rationing system. One told me how many high up law abiding citizens became his best customers.

The meat or goods were stored in the shed at his premises, and he would get a phone call from a local inspector to say: "Oh by the way we will be around to your place on such and such a date, to inspect your premises", so he always knew when the inspection was to take place and he had ample time to hide the evidence. Once the inspection was over and the premises declared operationally legal, the inspection team would move on to it next location, meanwhile at this location it was back to black market dealings until the next inspection notification was issued.

It's many years since I retired from farming and I have lost touch with the dealers I knew so well but I will never forget those characters of the agricultural trading world.

In this story I have mentioned the old railway system, and the cattle traders, but of course there were many other types of dealers all involved with farming and maybe I will describe some of them in another issue.

A time long ago, but not forgotten.

A Passer By.

A BOY AND THE HUNTER

I was about 7 years old at the time and I was riding home in the car with Mum after she had picked up my older sisters from the Blue School in Wells. On entering the lane that led up to the farm, I noticed all these rabbits, dozens of them, some sat on the edge of the road, and some lying in the road as if they had been struck with shock. I will always remember the look of their heads and eyes, all puffed up and the look of emptiness and despair, all very frightening to a small boy from the countryside where all animals appeared to be healthy and vibrant.

This was my first introduction to a disease called Myxomatosis, it was a disease which I later learnt was a type of pox virus that only effects rabbits. It was first discovered in 1896 in Uruguay and was imported to Australia in 1951 to control its large rabbit population initially having the desired, devastating effect. The disease was apparently illegally introduced to France and appeared in Britain in 1953. Talk at the time was that it was released in the countryside by government officials to cull the over population of rabbits, although this was never admitted or proven. It is spread by blood sucking insects in particular the rabbit flea, it is very infectious and almost wiped out the rabbit population. This disease kept recurring and still effects rabbits to this day, although it is rarely seen now.

I pick up my story 8 years after the decimation of the rabbit population and the rabbits had returned to the countryside in fewer but considerable numbers, no rabbits had been recently found with symptoms of the previous plague, so we are now in a period of history where rabbits are back and on the menu in many homes.

I had to cycle to school which I attended in Wells, a total of six miles there and back, summer and winter. I wonder how many children would contemplate this today, and also would it be safe? Not so many cars on the road then and also our hands where free from ipods, mobile phones and head phones that cyclists wear while cycling today, all to my mind very hazardous. In those days the drivers of cars used their car horns with enthusiasm to warn cyclists of their approach - when was the last time you used your car horn?

However back to my tale.

It was while I was cycling through Wells High Street that I noted that Mr Porch the butcher had rabbits hanging outside his shop for sale. Rabbits were obviously back in fashion and it was this opportunity that inspired me to become a hunter, also I could see an opportunity to subsidise my meagre pocket money.

I informed my dad of my plans, and he was aware of a company in a village called Misterton near Crewkerne, that manufactured rabbit snares. Fortunately for me, Dad said he would sponsor my venture and my elder sister was friendly with a farmer's son from Crewkerne so he obtained for me the snares needed.

I was not very successful at first but after some valuable lessons on how to set a snare from old Mr Diment who worked for Dad on the farm, who by the way also taught me how to paunch a rabbit and prepare it for sale, that I began to reap the rewards. Mr Diment also taught me how to hunt rabbits by using a ferret and nets but that another story.

So, loaded up with rabbits dangling from my handlebars I headed off to school and on arriving at the shop old Mr Porch eyed me with suspicion and demanded how I had obtained the goods for sale and where they free from the plague. I explained who I was, where the rabbits came from and yes, free of the disease. Probably more comforting for Mr Porch to know who my dad was. Dad used to have a milk round in Wells, before he sold it to Mr and Mrs Ruff, so he was well known in the community. I still believe it was the influence of who my dad was, and the respect he held in the Wells community rather than my business skills that secured my first business deal, but not bad I thought for a fifteen year old boy.

That first consignment of fresh rabbits, swelled my coffers to the tune of half a crown, which today would have the spending power of £5.00 and led on to many more sales.

I also sold mushrooms when in season to the chef at the Swan Hotel in Sadlers Street, I cannot remember what I got paid for them, but I will always remember the chef saying he used the skin and the stems for the soup. I wonder if they still do that today?

My business in the supply of fresh wild rabbit was brought to an abrupt end when the plague returned to the countryside and my goods where no longer saleable, so I picked up all my snares and hung them up in the shed, maybe to be used another day. However, from my adventure, I learnt valuable lessons and early business skills.

Interesting Times.

A Passer By.

A BOY AND DEFENCE

You may remember that I told you about a field called Forty Acres that we kids had to cross over on our walks to Wells, the one before we crossed over the railway line. Well, this field has its own story to tell and this is just one small part of its history.

After the evacuation of the British Army at Dunkirk, between 27th of May and 4th of June 1940 during World War Two, it was forced to leave all of its equipment behind, but the evacuation saved the men who would form the basis of a new army that would fight another day with new equipment and arms to safeguard our future independence as a sovereign nation.

Immediately after this evacuation it was decided to build a static line of defensive fortifications across the UK to halt or at least hold up any invasions by the German army, planned under the German operation Sea Lion. The defensive lines were planned under the leadership of General Sir Edmund Ironside, the newly appointed Commander-in-Chief, Home Forces.

The defence line that ran through this field was part of the Taunton Stop Line; this line ran north to south for over fifty miles across Somerset, Dorset and Devon. It ran from the northern end of the Taunton Stop Line near Highbridge along the river Brue, across the Mendips, from Wells and following the railway line from Maesbury into the Wellow Valley.

When it was possible, natural geographical barriers were used such as railway lines, especially constructed within cuttings and deep rivers, supported by numerous pill boxes that were constructed at regular intervals, such as at road and railway bridges. The Pill Box Defences, manned by soldiers of the Home Guard with heavy machine-guns that were supposed to stop any enemy advances until-reinforcements could be mobilised, fortunately their worth was never tested.

When the defence line got close to Wells, the rivers were too shallow to stop tanks, so trenches had to be excavated, huge trenches. A local eyewitness told me it was about three metres deep and nine metres wide, (ten feet and thirty feet in old money) called a tank trap trench. It ran across the field I called Forty Acres, across the lay-by that is sited on the Dulcote road as you leave Wells. The trench ended here as the underground rock made excavations impossible so they constructed huge blocks from concrete which were placed through the fields - again my eyewitness tells me they were about 2.4 metres by 2.4 metres, large enough to stop a tank and sited close enough together to stop tanks passing around them.

The trench that crossed the road to North Wootton, just past the cottage by the river and before you reach Browne's Garden Centre, was not excavated but a large concrete and steel girder barrier was constructed that could be placed across the road should it be required. There was also a pill box sited there but I think it may have been demolished when the trench was filled in after hostilities in Europe ended.

My eyewitness tells me that the trench was filled and landscaped as soon as peace was declared by an excavation company called Wheaton, from Chard.

We kids did not get to see the trench as by this time all traces of it were gone. It's amazing how nature has a way of self-healing.

The concrete blocks between Dulcote and Dinder were still in place and we used to play on and around them until they were later bulldozed into the woods at Dinder by a huge machine. If you go to the wood near Dinder you may still be able to find them.

The pill boxes were numerous and we kids had great fun exploring the insides of them, access was gained from a small doorway at the rear, down a few steps into the cavern which contained concrete seats, shelves, and several slits in the walls, through which the defenders could engage with the invader and we tried to imagine what it must have been like for the men that manned them.

From what I have seen from films and documentaries made about pill boxes I have come to the conclusion that although they were large and sturdy, they were perhaps not the safest of havens to be in during a committed attack from a well-armed infantry, let alone if they were accompanied by heavy tanks.

By the time we kids were old enough to explore them they had been abandoned for several years and were already showing signs of deterioration and I wondered if perhaps some of them had been built with inferior bricks and concrete due to the material shortages at the time. I don't know how they would have stood up to being shot at by a large Panzer tank but thank God they were never put to the test and men from the local Home Guard defence regimen did not have to defend them.

Also, up in the woods above Dulcote we discovered an underground shelter, the sides and roof constructed out of heavy curved corrugated steel sheets. This in turn was covered in soil to camouflage it and I guess make it bomb proof. It was below ground level and covered in young tree saplings, so it was only luck that we stumbled onto it during a walk. The entrance was discovered through a small opening at one end of the structure.

The inside measurements were about 8 metres long and about 2.5 metres wide, I think it was used by the Home Guard, or the secret army that was based in Somerset but I'm not sure. Whatever its intended use it became a fantastic secret den that we kids played in during the school summer holidays.

The fun and the interest that exploring these objects which were constructed in haste to save the realm and my interest in the organisation that created them, led me on to get involved in Defence myself and at the age of 14 I was recruited into an organisation called the Civil Defence Corps, the stories of my adventures with this organisation, I will tell you another day.

The Past that Defended our Future.

A Passer By.

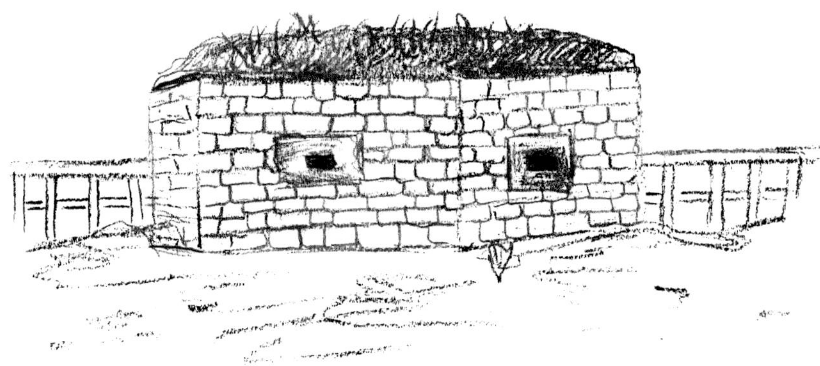

A BOY AND TUNA 170

From memory I think it was about 1966 and to date my only nautical experience was travelling from Weston-Super-Mare to Cardiff with my aged aunt some 5 years previously, on the S.S. Waverley - oh and of course that disastrous mackerel fishing trip with my dad when I became sea sick as the small craft left the harbour at Lyme Regis and I remained incapacitated for the whole voyage.

So how did I manage to be snared into this new adventure? I will have to leave it to you readers to decide. I suppose you have to bear in mind I was the youngest of five siblings, two of whom were brothers and I guess at the time I was influenced by their thinking, plus the ideas of my older friends and associates.

I cannot remember how I managed to become a fully paid up member of the syndicate who owned a small boat and that I was expected to pay my equal share of the expenses which if I remember were quite significant, but I was determined not to be seen as whinging weakling younger brother who appeared to have no imagination or sense of adventure. Anyway, what could go wrong on Blagdon Reservoir?

So, there you have it, I'm now a fully paid up nautical adventurer, the small craft was fitted with what was called a Seagull outboard motor and performed perfectly, especially on the safety of an inland lake.

These pleasurable days spent on the lake did not last long, not at all adventurous enough for my older shipmates who had already cast their eyes on greater navigational experiences and excitement.

So, it wasn't long before the boat trailer was attached to a friend's van and was headed towards that great nautical playground: Lyme Regis with its small harbour and of course that expanse of water called Lyme Bay.

The trailer was lowered down the steep launching ramp, the stern nudged into the salty water and away. The trusty Seagull outboard was attached, we climbed aboard, the starter rope was pulled and we glided across the harbour destined on another adventure.

We exited the harbour mouth under the watchful eyes of the local fishermen who were unloading the early morning catch, I wondered what was going through their minds as they saw a motley crew of young farmers venturing out into the notorious Lyme Bay without one single life belt among us! So, with such a prepared expedition, what could go wrong?

Well, all was good, we kept close to the shore, no point in taking unnecessary risks, anyway from this prime position we could eye up all the local girls sunbathing. Then Brian who was older and more experienced decided it was time to move further out to sea. He said it was time to test the boat's stability and our own resolve and this could only come from moving to deeper waters and in fairness all went to plan, until that is, the trusty Seagull outboard that had run with superb efficiency, decided to cough and die.

Now one of the first things that happen when a boat loses motion is that the sea takes command and you begin to toss up and down and start to drift out to sea carried by offshore currents, well you can imagine we all soon began to get increasingly worried to say the least.

Brian could not see any problem, after all he was a mechanic, "I'll just remove the plug clean it up and we will be away". Encouraging news indeed, that was until the hot plug burnt his hand and he let go of it and then proceeded to bounce off the side of the boat on its journey towards the ocean bottom. Brian quick as a flash reached out caught and the plug just off the surface of the water and tipped it into the bottom of the boat to cool off.

Well as I'm here to tell the tale, the plug was cleaned and dried and with a sharp pull of the starter cord we were on our way back to the sanctuary of the harbour, past the unsuspecting fishermen. We approached the landing slope with what can only be described as too much oomph, the keel hit the ramp, the boat swung around, and the propeller hit the concrete with so much momentum that it sheared off completely.

I climbed out of the boat onto dry land and swore I would never go to sea again! I have to say that my fellow sea men did go out many more times without mishap, but it was not for me, I'm definitely a land lubber!

It was soon afterwards that my associates decided it was time to get a bigger boat. I tried hard to convince them that the best way forward was to sell and cut our losses, for I had lost all enthusiasm. Well, I was told by the majority of shareholders that I was unlikely to salvage any funds and fell for the story that I would be much better off if I stuck with the others in this new venture, especially if a bigger and more valuable vessel was purchased and any way, when we finally sell out, we would have more valuable assets to realise. Well, I stayed with it, trusting my peers' advice, and the belief that in the future, second hand boats would, when we sell ours, be worth their weight in gold. I first laid my eyes on Tuna 170 as she lay at anchor in Bristol Harbour, she was about 8 m long and about 3 m wide, and had been crafted out of an old ship's life boat, so was probably very sea worthy, and it came complete with anchor, mast, and a large marine engine.

Negotiations were entered into with her current owner and a deal was struck; only problem now is how you transport an 8m boat from Bristol to Weymouth which was the only destination that had cheaper Harbour Dues.

Fortunately, we were all farmers' sons and our fathers over the years had purchased numerous tractors and farm machinery from a local merchant who was also a boat man himself with a large sea-going cruiser berthed at Weymouth.

He was very enthusiastic in our venture and offered his large low loader complete with driver to carry out the transportation to our neighbour's farm where we intended to spend the winter months working on our new purchase.

We were advised that to keep what is called a clinker built boat out of the water all that time would render in their wisdom so the boat was delivered straight to Weymouth Harbour.

Well, if you have ever owned or part owned a boat, you will know that they become a mistress of expense and hard labour. We spent most weekends working on her appearance which involved numerous hours of rubbing down old paintwork and applying layers of expensive marine paint bought from the local chandler's shop and to add to it all, harbour dues had to be paid promptly each month.

Brian managed to salvage a second-hand lorry engine from a scrap yard to replace the marine engine which proved to be completely seized up, something to do with sea air and salt water so I was told.

Anyway, the engine was lowered in via a makeshift crane that was bolted to the back of a land rover, all connections made including fuel, coolant system, and finally and most important, the prop shaft.

We untied her for the first time after her refurbishment and headed out to sea, lowering the mast so that we could navigate the low road bridge that spans the harbour.

It was a great experience. She handled well and was very sea worthy and with the huge engine she could face all that Weymouth Bay could throw at her. All was good, finally we had something to enjoy and spent many weekends enjoying ourselves, that was until...!!

Something was bound to go wrong and it did, spectacularly.

One day, I was down at the harbour on my own to spend a day sitting on the boat as that is what boat people do, trouble was, I could not find her anywhere in the harbour. After a search I went to the harbour master's office to make enquiries, and it was then that he told me the woeful tale.

Apparently, a boat owner from the neighbouring mooring had difficulty navigating out of his berth so he moved Tuna 170 to the edge of the dock and tied her up to a large metal mooring ring, failing afterwards to return her to her mooring line.

That night there was a large spring tide and Tuna 170 was unable to rise as she was secured to the land. As a result, as the tide came up Tuna 170 being unable to rise, the side of the boat attached went below water and the sea flooded in sending her to the bottom of the dock! Despite the attempts by the harbour master and others to untie her it was unsuccessful and she was doomed. What a disaster, there she was lying at peace about 6 ft below the surface.

Now, you may think that was the end of that but to a bunch of farmers' sons it was now a challenge to get her sea worthy. The arrival of all these lads in land rovers booted in wellies, loaded to the gunnels with winches, chains, ropes, shackles, anything useful that could be found lying around the farm, must have been quite a spectacle to the locals who arrived, sat on the wall had picnics, and cheered us on with banter and not always appreciated advice.

Next to where she lay was berthed a large side paddle steam ship. I'm unable remember its name, but being in for a refit and her lifeboats removed, she became the stable platform to mount operations.

We winched chains underneath our craft and secured them to the steamer's life boat launching rigging, very useful as they contained the most important ingredient - winches and large ones at that.

Slowly we used these winches to bring up the wreck and as soon as she broke water the pumps we had hired locally were brought forward with great effect, and as they say, 'up she rises'. Well, we were pleased, the Harbour Master was pleased to have the wreck removed from his harbour bed and spectacle over, the crowd dispersed.

To end the tale, Tuna 170 never went back to sea under our ownership, she was sold at what I remember was a great financial loss, but look, no one died and we were thankful for that.

The consortium of owners was disbanded and we returned to what we knew best, working on the land and feeding the nation. Nowadays when I go to Weymouth I always think of Tuna 170 and wonder what became of her.

To go to sea or not go to sea - that is the question.

A Passer By.

A BOY AND CIVIL DEFENCE – PART ONE

I was sitting in the classroom only half listening to the English literature teacher who was trying to convince us that there would be no worthwhile future out in the adult world unless we were fully conversant with the great masters of literature, without whom life would be empty of culture. I sat there wondering why the Education Authority thought it was so important that I, who was destined to be a farmer's boy, would need any influence from Dickens or Shakespeare to make me a better farmer, or person in society come to that.

I however, was looking out of the window more interested in the pair of magpies that were constructing a nest in the tree next to the school playing field and realising that they did not find it necessary to have instruction or lectures from some Master Magpie on construction methods. It appeared to me that they just knew how to do it, like being instructed by some inherited educational gene that is installed in all of us when we are created.

My grandfather on my mother's side was a Master Builder, and I discovered in later life that I was able to lay brick and stone in a professional manner without any instruction of any kind. I just knew how to do it and I'm confident that many of you who are reading this will recognise what I am saying. However back to what I was supposed to be telling you about the Civil Defence Corp.

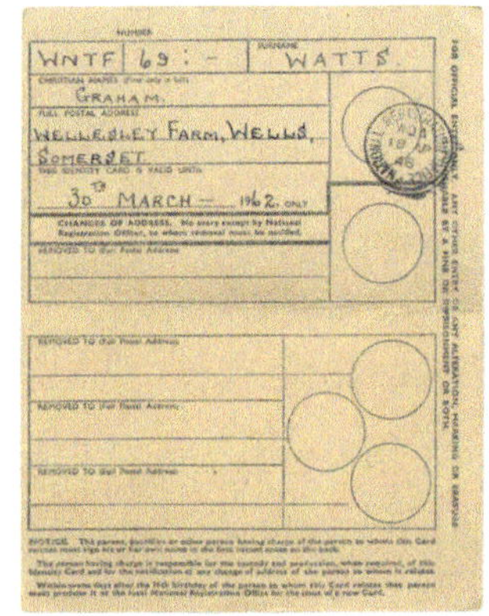
NUMBER
WNTF 69 : -
SURNAME
WATTS.
CHRISTIAN NAMES (first only in full)
GRAHAM.
FULL POSTAL ADDRESS
WELLESLEY FARM, WELLS,
SOMERSET.
THIS IDENTITY CARD IS VALID UNTIL
30th MARCH — 1962. ONLY
CHANGES OF ADDRESS. No entry except by National Registration Officer, to whom removal must be notified.
REMOVED TO (full Postal Address)
REMOVED TO (full Postal Address)
REMOVED TO (full Postal Address)
REMOVED TO (full Postal Address)

My concentration on the activity of those magpies was broken by a loud report on the classroom door and on enquiry it was the Head Master who was accompanied by this gentleman dressed in a military uniform who informed us that the school was to undertake instruction on Civil Defence as an extracurricular activity and we could drop a subject to participate. I immediately dropped English literature from my future education.

I cannot remember what rank this officer was but he was probably a Deputy Chief Rescue Officer of the organisation he was representing and he was also possibly a volunteer.

The Civil Defence was founded in 1935 and operated as such until 1945 when the war ended, then in 1949 a new version was adopted, (I joined in 1961). The C.D.C was finally stood down in 1968, and it was changed in 1949, as it was decided that as the next war would be nuclear then a whole new approach had to be initiated to training and operations.

Younger readers may not be aware that when I was a boy America and Russia were what is called sabre rattling and everyone thought Nuclear War would eventually take place, so all sorts of nuclear bunkers were being constructed in all counties. These were not designed to keep the public safe but were Command Centres for all the services activated into response after an attack had taken place.

My part in the great scheme of things was to be trained to assist in picking up the pieces after the event of a nuclear attack on Bristol with a five-megaton bomb. Rescue in Bristol would not have been contemplated as it would have been completely destroyed, along with all its inhabitants.

Taking a line as the crow flies, Radstock would almost be totally destroyed but leave some survivors down here in Wells. Although severe damage would be caused, there would be many survivors who needed immediate rescue from blast and fire damaged houses.

One of the questions in my exam paper was in the scenario that you arrive on the scene and it is reported to you that there are houses severely damaged and contain survivors who are severely injured and need immediate rescue and attention; also, at the same time there is a bunker full of uninjured locals but they are trapped inside by debris: Who do you rescue first? The answer is the bunker, as the uninjured from the bunker could assist you under instruction to rescue the injured. Makes sense when you think about it.

At the tender age of 14 years, I was faced with this great responsibility and decided that I wanted to be part of this great organisation that had been set up to assist others and I was looking forward to the training sessions that I had committed myself to.

I, as a country lad, could still go searching for birds' nests, and climbing trees with my mates from school, visiting the old quarry, where we had great adventures and just growing up in this vast playground that nature had laid at my feet, but I now know that the C.D.C, was the vehicle that assisted and inspired me most during that journey from childhood to becoming an adult.

My first active training was in communications and we underwent instruction on how to lay temporary telephone cables and connect them to phones located in the back of the communication land-rovers. The land-rovers also carried long thin wooden poles to be used to elevate and support the cables across roadways.

The bell was actuated at the other end by an electrical signal, this was achieved by turning the handle that was attached to the side of the telephone. It was great fun when we would ask a raw recruit to hold the terminals to see if they were working, and they would be awarded with and electric shock not unlike the one received from a car spark plug. All recruits went through this initiation in communications, including myself, apparently, all part of the bonding process.

Radio was used only to communicate with other organisations working in the same areas and we had to learn all the call signs etc; however, I could not get my head around Morse Code and always had great difficulty in this aspect of communications.

Communications was interesting but not half as much fun as firefighting. Now this I really enjoyed! We were issued with what is called a stirrup pump; this was a small piece of equipment but was very efficient when fighting small fires. The pump was not unlike a hand pump and was activated by raising and pushing down a handle that was attached to a plunger inside a metal tube from the base of which was attached a long rubber hose. This in turn was attached to a metal tube which contains a small nozzle which ejected the water at high pressure.

At the training site a brazier was filled with paper and wood made aggressive by adding paraffin and this was placed inside a concrete bunker reconstructed as a room in a house and set on fire.

It took two personnel to fight the fire, one to operate the pump and one to direct the water onto the fire. The operator with the hose would crawl on his stomach as close to the fire as the heat allowed, he was on his stomach to avoid the smoke, at which point he would shout the command, 'water on!'. When the fire was extinguished the command was,' water off!'. A very efficient piece of kit and was great fun to operate.

At the age of 15, I qualified as a competent emergency part-time fireman and I was very proud of the fact and would love to have the opportunity to enjoy such an experience, but I don't know how it would be achieved nowadays. They wouldn't be allowed to touch the equipment for the fear of breaking a nail, let alone be placed in the position of attacking a live fire.

This is the end of part one of my story due to space, but if you want more, I will send in part two next month - times of youth and fear of future Hostilities.

A Passer By.

A BOY AND SEASONAL VISITORS

I suppose the first indication that our seasonal visitors where on their way was the month of April giving way to the first week in May, and the seasonal call of the Cuckoo as they looked to invade unsuspecting hosts to foster their brood.

The next was undoubtable the sound of the clip clop of multiple hooves, and the grind of metal wheels as they crushed the loose gravel that lay on the farm lane, and the constant rattle of cooking utensils as they banged against the side of the colourful caravans, it was the time of the annual migration of the gypsy families.

These families I am told but have no reliable proof, were thought to be the descendants of the Famous Gypsy, Granny Issaacs, who were making their way to the large layby that was situated on the top lane above the farm, there to set up camp, and settle down for usually about a week, or so.

The gypsy ladies would come down to the farm to fill up their tin buckets with fresh water from the old hand pump that lived in mothers wash room situated in the lean-to attached to the farm house.

Granny Issaacs I was told was the queen of the gypsies and when she passed away, was cremated along with her caravan, somewhere near Bristol, according to the ancient custom.

Their arrival always coincided with the May Fair that took place on the first Saturday of May which was hosted in the old cattle market in Wells. (The site now of the Bus Station)

The Gypsy families gathered at the fair in large numbers, not just from our site but multiple sites set up in and around St Cuthbert's out parish, their business there was to trade horses, with other Gypsy families and local farmer. As I remember as a child there were not many horses as by now tractors had taken the place of horses, but still a few farmers kept horses for local chores, and liked to think they could pick up a bargain.

A local farmer told me that you had to careful in what you bought, as it was believed by some that that the sellers used to bleed there horses previous to sell, as it was thought that the

new blood created, made the horses to appear young and virial.

The wives of the horse traders would sell heather that was probably gathered from the Quantocks, and also the famous Gypsy Clothes pegs, and of course to the believer if you crossed their palms with silver they would attempt to enlighten you on your future.

Mum had a bag full of these gypsy made pegs, but would always buy a few more each year, just in case they were needed, I think these very efficient pegs went out of fashion when someone invented the smaller spring loaded pegs which we are familiar with today.

After all the trading was completed the Gypsies would retire to the Mermaid Inn that was situated in Tucker Street, there to consume large amounts of ale as they celebrated the good fortunes of their trading, unfortunately although they all entered the pub in good humour, after a few hours the peace was broken by loud shouting, as many of them fell from the local bar intent on beating each other senseless. Order was only restored when the local bobby arrived and laid down the law, at which point the Gypsies would return to the bar to continue the celebrations. I'm not sure whether there was a genuine grievance between them or they just got boisterous, and actually enjoyed it.

Then late at night they would return to their caravans some sat two to a horse, some with loud banter, and some singing, as the horses plodded onwards, without navigation from there riders back to the sanctuary of the beautifully painted Caravans.

We children were scared of the Gypsies, as during the year if we misbehaved Mum and Dad would say if we didn't behave we would be given to the Gypsies, you imagine parents saying that to kids today, the parents would probably be fined and the children sent for counselling from social services.

However despite the threat of capture, or being given in to slavery, my brothers and I took strength from each other and went close to the camp to satisfy our curiosity, and to our surprise we were made welcome by the Gypsy children who I think were as curious of us as we of them. We entered the sanctuary of the Gypsies with awe, and stayed close together for support, some of the adults there were sultry and unfriendly, but by comparison most were friendly, and we were even invited to dine with them, but after one look into the greasy pot that simmered over the open fire we declined the offer.

There was one old man who was sat on a porcelain toilet that was not connected to any main sewer, Obviously relieving himself, and reading a paper, we found this most amusing.

One old lady told us that when available Hedgehog was a good dish, and was prepared by covering the animal with wet clay, and then setting on the hot coals of the fire to simmer, when the clay was broken the prickles came away with the clay and you were left with a tasty dish.

There was another guy who was cutting nut hazel sticks into short lengths and then splitting them down the center into two equal halves, after some whittling with a sharp knife the two halve were joined back together with a short piece of tin cut from an old tin can and secured with a single small nail, and hey presto you had a gypsy clothes peg.

There was not always enough feed for the horses that grazed on the side of the road, so their owners used to put them in Dads fields late at night, and then collect them early before he got up to go milking.

Dad got wise to this and one morning he was at the gate before the horse owners had chance to sneak them out, he demanded compensation and thought that things might get a bit awkward, but to his surprise one of the gypsies put his hand in his pocket brought out a pound note and handed it to dad with an apology, so that shows that although they took liberties, if found out they were prepared to compensate.

They also used to sell dogs to unsuspecting punters, and it is said that when they packed up to leave one of them went to the dogs new owners house at night, called to the dog, and it would run to the voice it recognised, and was available to sell again another day.

The bulldozer that destroyed dads orchards at the same time also pushed out the hedge, and dad converted the old lay-by into part of his field and fenced it off from the highway, so that was the end of the migration of the Gypsies to the farm.

This story is written from my memories as a child, and stories I have been told by others, and is written without prejudice.

Different times, many memories.

A Passer By.

THE OLD QUARRIES

I looked down on the ancient scene from the comfort of the JCB cab, sheltered from the cold spring wind that can blow with no remorse across the Mendip Hills. I have to say at that time in the early 1970s, the cab had no heater or come to that any form of air conditioning, apart from opening a window, but it was an improvement on the old machine that had no cab at all, and you were open to all elements.

I was in an ancient quarry at Chelynch which is not far from Shepton Mallet on the Frome road. Quarries like this had been in production since Roman Times, at least 2000 Years, the product they produced was Oolitic Limestone.

This type of stone was used for construction work, it was durable and easy to carve so was used in abundance in old cathedrals, churches and manor house construction. If you look at it under a microscope it consists of round particles of sand that had rolled around the ancient seabed millions of years ago and had adhered together to form the rock I'm talking about.

Why was I there? Well. I was hired by the quarry owners to excavate the "over burden" so that the valuable stone could be exposed.

At this time the method of removing the stone had not really changed for centuries, the stone was in natural layers of about one metre thick but tended to vary over different parts of the quarry. Between each layer was a layer of natural sand, it was called a sand fault and it enabled the large stones, which could weigh up to a ton or more in weight to be removed in one piece.

First the quarrymen had to drill a line of holes across the back and on one side of the stone to be removed. Once this had been achieved tapered metal chisels where place in each hole, these where then driven in with heavy hammers, moving across all positions until the stone would crack off at the desired place.

The lifting crane on this site was a very ancient piece of equipment probably a vision of a Victorian engineer from somewhere up north, its moving parts were not unlike a

huge clock, massive big cogs partnered up with pinion gears, gears that were engaged through a large flywheel and clutch mechanism with huge long metal hand-held control levers. There was also foot control pedals so you can imagine the dexterity needed by the crane operator.

I think at this time it was electric powered but in the Victorian days it was no doubt powered by steam. It had a long Jib with pulleys through which a metal cable ran to service the lifting crook, it had no travelling wheels but was permanently mounted on a metal framework. I guess they had to dismantle the whole thing to move it around the quarry when it could no longer reach its working area.

Once the stone was free of Mother Earth, the crane was attached through a piece of mechanism called a Lewis, this was inserted into a pre-drilled hole and as the crane took the strain the Lewis would tighten up, and the stone would rise up to the top of the quarry, ready for dressing and transportation.

All large knobs and excrescences that were removed, the stone was dressed and taken away by truck to be ground up to make facing material for concrete blocks. This procedure was repeated over and over for each stone removed and every stone was slightly different in size shape and weight so each stone removed was treated as an individual.

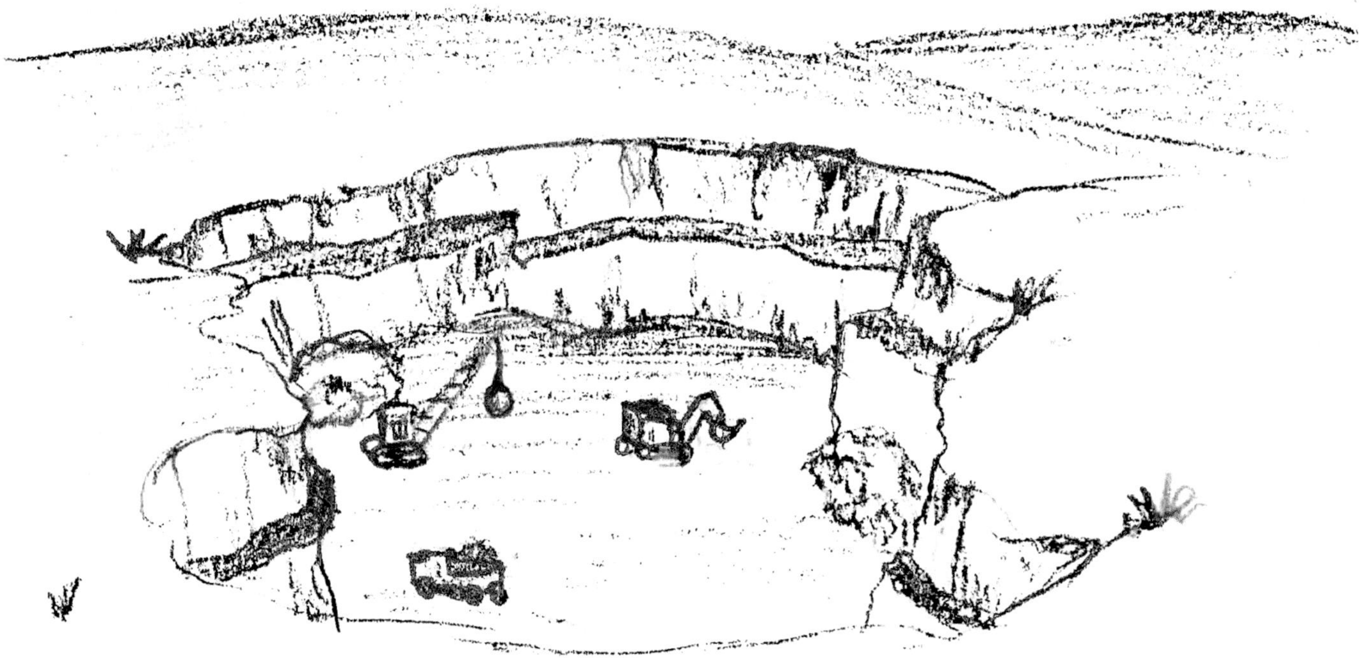

The three men who carried out this skilful work were a father and his son plus a labourer. Each knew their trade and were always aware of the position and safety of each other.

The father was the boss, and he was respected by his peers for his skill and safety conscience attitude. A quarry was a safe place only as long as everyone obeyed the rules especially on wet days when the stone and quarry floor was wet and slippery.

One day I placed a sledge hammer down with handle pointing towards the sky, the old fellow shouted at me, "Lay that hammer down flat you fool, if you leave it like that, someone could fall on it and injure themselves". I was chastised and was afraid to ask what would happen if someone fell over it when it was laid down, I had too much respect to do that.

A large circular saw was later installed in one of the old sheds to cut up some of the smaller stones into brick type building stones of various sizes to fill specialist order for building supplies.

The method of removing stones from a modern quarry has not changed that much but nowadays the stone is cut out with a large chainsaw type of equipment, and removed by large fork lift trucks. I don't know what the old quarry manager would have thought, he probably would have said something like: it's about bloody time life was made easier.

The quarry manager retired a few years later and his son moved on to work at one of the larger limestone quarries. I can't remember where the labourer went, however the quarry was soon closed down. It was reopened a few years later, whether it's still in operation I don't know.

What I do know is the many times I went to work at the quarry was very enjoyable. I have always worked with nature and at this place I was able to work with a very friendly bunch of operatives who were making use of just one type of material that nature had supplied and made available for the benefit of man.

A Passer By.

'The Forge' From left, Leonard Field living at Sunnyside, David Garland living at the Forge and Jack Plenty, the horse owner living Near Free Farm. A Posed Picture from the Wells Journal 1955.

THE FORGE

The chilly late summer wind of 2019 blew through the door of the old forge. The door handle, once shiny with constant use, was now beginning to dull and rust. The old container that once held valuable spares now being filled with redundant goods and spare parts - its next destiny would be the local scrap merchants' yard for disposal. The shelves once full of replacement spare parts and utilities slowly emptying as no replacements had been ordered.

The pile of new farm gates that had awaited customers over the years would soon be all gone, possibly with the old petrol pump that had served the neighbourhood for decades. The yard once full of machinery awaiting repair was notably absent, no Land Rovers containing impatient farmers bustling to get attention, each thinking their request for help was more important than their neighbour. The engineer proprietors conscious that each one of their customers were of equal standing and important to their business were trying to make sure that each customer left their premises content and relieved of their immediate needs.

This was the hub of the community the centre of collective knowledge, here all the local farmers exchanged local news and gossip with their neighbours, if you wanted the latest gossip, going to the forge was the instinctive thing to do.

However, the autumn years of the old family business has now arrived, time for the current caretakers of this old traditional icon to decide what is best for their future. Times have changed for this agricultural based business, all the small farmers have gone out of business, no longer do they require the need for the services and supplies from this specialist business. With no family members available to pick up the reins of this old dynasty maybe it's time for the proprietary family to reflect on what they had archived through decades of hard work serving the community and thinking (quite rightly in my opinion) and planning to move forwards to a long and awaited happy retirement.

THE BEGINNING

The peel rang out as hot iron was forged into shape on the old anvil by the skilful blows of the blacksmith, the ancient sound echoing off the old church wall heralding the arrival of Otto Garland who had moved to the village and was engaged in his ancient craft.

He married his wife Frances and arrived in North Wootton in 1904 rented a cottage in Tanyard Lane where 5 of his children were born.

He founded a workshop at the old Bark Mill, where he would continue to carry out his trade until 1930, apart from the years 1914 to 1919 when he served as a Blacksmith under His Majesty's service in France. While he was away to war, the tenancy expired so his wife in his absence in France bought a cottage at the end of Dark Lane, now the site of the current Forge (I'm informed) for the sum of Ten Pounds.

The cottage in Tanyard Lane was replaced by a bungalow many years later and is now the home of the children who were born in the cottage at Tanyard Lane, were; Walter, Lionel, Roland, Ivor, and Wilfred. However, David was born at the cottage in Dark Lane. Walter worked for a time for his father before moving to be a farmer at West Compton.

Lionel, suffering from eczema was unable to work at the Forge, so he became a taxi owner and operator, later to become landlord of the long lost Queen's Head Pub which he ran with his wife Nelly. The pub was situated in North Town, he was also proprietor of the farm that came with the pub tenancy.

Roland, nick-named Punch, was involved in arboriculture setting out new orchards around in Somerset, being involved setting out many Perry Pear orchards for the Showering Brothers who famed for the manufacture of Babycham. If you can find an older orchard in which every way you look the trees line up, then you can guarantee that it was planted by Punch Garland or by someone under his supervision.

Ivor, nick-named Ginger, left home to become the resident estate blacksmith for the Mendip Mental Health Hospital in Wells which was self-sufficient, owning several Farms.

Wilfred, who trained to be a wheelwright under his father's employment emigrated to New Zealand. So, the only son to take up and run the family business was David the youngest son.

DARK LANE

The forge situated in Dark Lane was constructed by Otto Garland in the early 1930s, it was of red brick construction with asbestos roof complete with a large built-in forge fire grate with a brick chimney leading out through the roof. The forge building contained all the machinery and tools needed to carry out the many tasks required of his customers. He supplied the manufacture of anything made from wrought iron and steel, especially the shoes for horses whose owners or grooms were regular customers.

There was specialist machinery for making metal tyres for carts and haywain's used by the local farmers and many other metal components needed by his customers around the locality. So, this is where Otto was further developing his business when he was joined in the business by his youngest son David.

David did not originally work in the family business. He was working away from home when in July 1939 at the age of 21 he was called to serve his country in the Second World War returning home after demob sometime in 1946.

David married Mary and moved into the then new house No.7 Church View, they were blessed with two sons Gordon, born 1947 and Douglas born 1951.

David was not a skilled engineer at this time but under the supervision of his skilful father, soon became an expert in all the trades needed to run this rural business. Otto died in 1953 ten years after his wife who died in 1943, they are both buried in the local church yard. David restored the old roof to the cottage and moved in with his wife Mary and the boys later in 1953.

During this time David continued in what might be described as a one man operation, but this did not impede the growth of the business. At this time, many farmers demanded water supplies to their fields, grant aided in those days. He was the man called to satisfy their need, he was probably responsible for most of the water installation and cattle troughs in the neighbourhood.

I remember visiting the Forge as a young boy with my father and watching the agricultural horses being fitted with new shoes by David the farrier and later I was intrigued while he was cutting new threads to plain metal water pipes with special dyes. His skill with the soldering iron was in great demand to repair holes in rusty milk pails that the farmers were reluctant to throw out. He was a skilful welder, oxygen and acetylene. Blow torch in hand there was very little that the farmers could break that he could not repair to pristine condition.

So here we have a very busy man with great dexterity looking to expand. This opportunity came to hand when his brother Lionel was able to purchase a small neighbouring paddock. A deal was struck and in 1956 David with land available was able to erect a new shed to incorporate the additional machinery needed, as the blacksmiths shop was slowly transforming into the agricultural engineering business.

Business continued to grow and by 1971 the extension was added to the original building doubling its size. The business was acquired many agencies during its growth including Gascoigne, milking equipment and Bamford agricultural machinery. He had the premises and he had the support of dozens of local faithful customers, what he needed now was help and support.

This came in earlier on when Gordon left school and after training at Radstock engineering college, joined his father in the business in the year 1963. By this time the business had extended to incorporate the supply and installation of milking parlours and other sophisticated farm appliances that where rapidly being developed and introduced in the agricultural workplace. Realising the needs of this new age, Gordon returned to college, and qualified as an electrician, a skill that was greatly needed in this expanding business.

A few years later more help was available as Douglas had left school and joined the firm, his speciality was plumbing, gas and electric welding. At this time, they had the biggest electric welder in the district and it had to have a special piece of equipment fitted to it to stop the lights flickering throughout the village when it was being operated, sometimes late in the evening during a busy summer. To the best of my knowledge it was around this time the company O.V Garland and Sons Ltd was incorporated.

In 1983 Gordon who was living in the company house in Wells moved into the cottage at the forge, at the same time David and Mary moved into the bungalow that now stands in Tanyard Lane on the site of the old rented cottage, but I must say David and Mary returned every day to assist and serve the growing customers.

In 1978 the forge building erected in 1930 was demolished, the site cleared and was excavated to provide the position for the new forecourt and electric petrol pump. Previous to this, petrol was delivered through an old antiquated hand pump. The petrol was hand pumped up into glass container and when filled to the correct volume was released through gravity into the vehicle or receptacle placed under its nozzle.

So, the years pass by and David not getting any younger, appoints Gordon to run the business as general manager and Douglas was promoted to the workshop and in the field repair manager, both boys accepting their separate responsibilities, worked well together.

With David now taking a back seat and work piling in, the brothers took on two more employees, one as general workshop repair man and another as a skilled boiler maintenance and repair specialist to service the large industrial steam boilers associated with the manufacturing companies on their books.

The company has continued to operate in a very efficient way and catered for the challenges presented by the fast evolutional changing agricultural industry.

In time, the Pilton Pop festival was created, (now known as Glastonbury Festival) and O.V Garland and Sons were leaders in creating the infrastructure. To this day Douglas is still respected by the festival for his leadership and knowledge on all water installation throughout the site.

David, who continued as church warden and parish councillor for many years died in 2006, followed by Mary in 2013 and both are interned in the local churchyard. After his death the business continued to trade until 2019.

As I said in my opening remarks, the autumn years of this long established local icon has arrived. I would like to thank Gordon for his help in my research and supply of photos; I trust the newcomers to the village will appreciate this story of a long lost legacy of the village.

I know that the older generation of readers of this magazine will and have their own fond memories.

A Passer By.

THE OLD ALLEY

As you leave the village of North Wootton on the Pilton Hill Road, you cannot miss the huge building sited on the edge of the crossroads, The Crossways Hotel - or is it an Inn, I'm not sure?

Well, it was not always like that, back in late sixties and early seventies it would have been described as a small village cider house or public Inn, sitting on its own site in the corner of an old cider orchard with its own cottage garden and collection of old sheds and buildings. It also had its own cider making facilities on site and in those days, it was called the Crossways Inn and Mr Green was the proprietor.

It was a haven for farmers, farm labourers and quarry men who frequented its facilities to quench their day long thirsts and catch up on the local gossip. It was basically a Cider House with additional beer and spirit sales; it consisted of three small rooms. The main bar contained beer barrels supported on timber trestles, and cider barrels supported upright on bricks or wood with taps protruding from their bases, metal drip trays were placed below to collect spillages, these spillages were usually fed to the pigs.

Beer glasses with large handles hung from hooks distributed around on the ceiling but in easy reach of a thirsty punter who would grab a glass, fill it with beer and or cider from the barrels and go and sit on a usually turned up empty beer crate if no chair was available. He would settle up with the landlord as he left.

Crisp packets were available complete with their own contained blue bag of salt, the crisps lived in the window sill in a large cardboard box, next to this was the washing up sink and wooden drainage board.

The next room was the card room complete with Welsh type settles, wooden chairs and a large kitchen type table, large enough for several games to be played simultaneously. Coinage was not allowed but you could win a lot of used matches. Next to that was a small room used for table skittles, shove halfpenny, and of course the dart board with wooden doors on which the scores were recorded with white chalk.

So, this was the local pub that I and many village boys and girls used to frequent in our younger days and many of us met our future wives and husbands there, it was the hub of village life.

One night I with some of the village lads and local characters were enjoying the beverage and hospitality when Mr Green asked us to leave early as he was feeling under the weather. We asked if he would be okay and he said he would sleep in the chair downstairs that night as he was afraid that if he went to bed he would not feel happy. Well, I don't know where he slept but it was announced that he had died that night and the pub was closed.

The Crossways Inn and the grounds in which it stood was put up for auction and was purchased by Mr Kirkham. His first name was Jack, but everyone knew him as John Kirkham. He with his wife at the time of the auction were the proprietors of the local public house called the Apple Tree, the tenancy of which they gave up when they embarked on a huge restoration and enlargement of the Crossways. This took place over several years, finally it evolved as the building you see today and it was during this time of development that I became involved.

I have to say that although the exterior appearance has not changed much, the interior has been restored and brought up to a superb high standard by its present owners. If you're going by, pop in and enjoy its superb hospitality and luxurious surroundings, have a word with Simon who has been employed there for many years and I'm sure will enlighten you on its history.

Some older residents of the village will remember that outside the pub where the steep walkway that leads to the porch way now stands, was sited a large, long wooden single story timber building. It had a pitched galvanised steel sheet roof, not unlike any old army accommodation hut, but inside this particular hut was a fine skittle alley, which as you know needs to be very level to give satisfaction to both home and away teams.

To achieve this the hut had been constructed upon brick pillars that were distributed at regular intervals along its length at different heights to compensate for the uneven site. Well, this structure was on the site that was required for the construction of the fine large kitchen building that Mr Kirkham was about to construct as part of the enlargement programme, so it had to go.

But now lies the problem, it had to be moved in one piece, not broken down, as it was to be moved to a new site in the car park and continue its life as a skittle alley, now if you have ever been in a skittle alley you can imagine how long this building was.

I was at this time involved in earth moving and ground working and had carried out small scale earth works on site so I suppose it was obvious that I would be approached to undertake this difficult operation, but I was not that confident. I suggested he employed a national crane operator to carry out this tricky operation which would involve lots of slings chains and heavy lifting equipment. His reply was they won't touch it because he had already contacted them, something to do with the unstable condition of the building, that had sat on its present site for decades and would probably not survive the excessive movement.

So, it was down to me and my team who were in my employ at the time, Mr Kirkham said "look have a go, if it falls apart we will have a bonfire, if not, perhaps we will have a celebration". So, there you have it, a building about 18 m long and about 3m wide was about to be moved. (Was 3 meters, right?)

I studied the problem and took a lesson from the old Egyptians, if they could move large objects using wooden rollers, why not me? I did have a few old telegraph poles lying around on the farm, so let's have a go.

I begged and borrowed as many hydraulic jacks as I could, these were employed to support the building, as the brick pillars were removed and slowly the building was lowered to the ground.

I abandoned the idea of telegraph poles as rollers as I discovered that a local farmer had recently purchased at auction some long metal tubes that in a previous life had supported radio masts. These turned out to be invaluable, the building was lowered onto them, a large wire rope was attached to the end of the building, the other end was attached to a large tracked vehicle.

The tractor took the strain and with bated breath the building slowly moved forward, as it moved more rollers were placed in front to follow its already predicted route of travel to its new site.

This particular building proved to be very strong being timber built, probably of seasoned timber such as red deal, teak, or even cedar, it arrived at its new home in perfect condition. With a puffed up chest and a regal air I entered the building, the clock was still in its place on the wall recording perfect time, I picked up a skittle ball and sent it down the alley with the confidence of the conqueror, when a plan has come together.

That night Mr Kirkham arranged a skittle night for me and my team, to show his appreciation and if I remember a few free pints and bread and cheese were enjoyed by all. We had worked hard that day and had achieved what we had set out to do and believe me we played hard all that night.

I have to give full credit to that team of workers that worked with dedication and harmony and each contributed with ideas to overcome problems as and when they occurred. Always believe in yourself, confidence is a must, adapt and overcome.

The old alley was used for many years thereafter, only to fall into decline and made obsolete by the construction of a new internal skittle alley. It was used as a storage building for many years and was finally removed when the present car park was enlarged.

I hope you enjoyed this little story of local history, if history is not recorded we may lose our heritage.

I'm sure some of the more senior members of our village may have different and personal memories of the past life, here in the village, this is just a record of my own memories.

Just another small moment in history.

A Passer By.

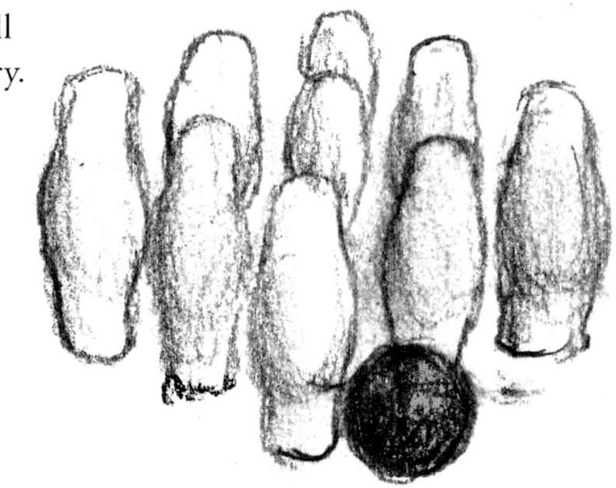

THE MINING EXPERIENCE (GOING UNDERGROUND)

The explosion when it came was louder than expected. The high velocity sound bounced off the ancient rock face and ran down the ancient valley to come to rest against the redundant paper mill. Lumps of Dolomitic Conglomerate and Limestone flew through the air at supersonic speed and left scars and scrapes on the canopy of the trees that grew in the valley bottom, while the lacerated leaves fell like snow to come to rest on the bottom of the ancient river that had flowed out of the cave and ran down past the mill to disgorge into the River Axe for centuries. The senior engineer of the project was heard to comment to his fellows, that perhaps too much explosive was used; this will have to be remedied in the future.

It was early summer 1974 and a team of miners had been made redundant in the coal mines of Somerset and who had recently been recruited by a private mining company. They had arrived on site to construct a tunnel through the ancient rock face and navigate it to its destination, which was a large cave cavern that had been previously discovered by scuba divers navigating up the underground course of the stream that rose up in the Mendips. It would eventually exit through the cave mouth at Wookey Hole.

The ancient handmade paper mill had long closed and in 1973 Madame Tussauds had purchased the site which included the Wookey Hole Cave attraction.

My family at this time owned a contracting and plant hire company and we had been contacted by the mining company to supply a suitable track vehicle, capable of opening up the valley floor to give construction equipment access to the work site. This machine would remain on site all the summer months to assist in the logistics of the operation.

It became obvious in the early days that although the constructed temporary roadway was a good route to and from the site it would be unsuitable for the transportation of the tonnes of blasted rock that would have to be removed from site. Fortunately for the miners there was an ancient leat that had been constructed in the old days to collect water from the cave mouth and transport it to give power to the old mill.

The leat had been constructed quite high up in the valley side and fortunately the bank constructed by the Ancients to support and retain the volumes of water safely, was recognised as being wide enough and engineered to a standard to provide suitable site as an additional exit route.

A small train arrived on site with several dump trucks, accompanied by a suitable quantity of narrow gauge rail track. The miners constructed the track along the bank of the Leat from the work site to the dump zone which was sited in the old car park, all constructed by hand, and with only the aid of winches and crow bars manhandled the train and its trucks up the side of the bank and onto the previously laid tracking.

This was an unbelievable achievement those miners were as strong as oxen and ingenious when overcoming obstacles, the charge hand would say find a solution and the problem will disappear and they usually did.

Once the line was operational a large turntable had to be constructed outside the tunnel site to enable the train to be turned around, this was constructed with sweat, and large bulks of heavy timbers overlaid with heavy timber planking. Once this entire infrastructure was in place mining could commence.

The site of the proposed drill holes was marked out on the rock face and once the Project Manager was happy with the positioning, the drilling could commence.

The direction and position of the drill holes were very important; the first few holes were about 300mm apart and were drilled at such an angle that at the back of the section the holes would meet, thus forming a triangular section. The drillers worked their way out towards the outside edge altering the drilling angle a few degrees, so that the perimeter holes were put in straight. I forget how wide the excavation was but it had to be at least 3 metres.

Once all drilling was completed the holes were charged with explosive, now this is the clever bit, each section of explosive had a detonator that was timed to set the charge off a few nanoseconds from its predecessor, thus you had like a sound like roll of thunder rather than a solid blast.

What was happening was the first charge would blow out a wedge, the next charge would blow its debris inwards and outwards into the void created by the previous and so on and so on until a tunnel was created about 3 meters deep, and 3 meters wide round in shape but flat at it base.

Next came the removal of the debris. This was achieved by the use of a small train-like vehicle which had a shovel attached to it. The operator who rode the machine would drive forwards and load the bucket and once filled the bucket would fly over the machine and deposit the spoil into an awaiting train truck, this in turn when full would be replaced by an empty one awaiting on the turn table. Once all trucks and the excavation was free of debris, the train would trundle down the track to the dump site.

Now the drilling could restart, this process had to be repeated every time the tunnel moved forwards towards its goal. If after blasting the roof of the excavation was good and safe, so be it, but if not, it had to be supported by resin secured bolts and the rock grouted with liquid cement which was injected under high pressure.

Navigation was very important; the route of the tunnel had been previously worked out by engineers. I'm not sure how the miners navigated their route but from memory they attached a piano wire with a weight attached to form a plumb bob to the roof of the tunnel, then as they moved forwards they added more. Once the first two were in line, from this line site they were able to navigate where the next plum bob should be positioned, thus following some predetermined route.

After many months the tunnel reached its target and the ancient subterranean cavern was breached. I was lucky enough to be on site that day and was one of the first people to witness this achievement. It was very dark and the only light we had were mining lamps and one spot lamp that had been rushed to the site. Access was by a ladder down onto what can only be described as a sandy beach that lay alongside the ancient underground river. On the sandy beach was an old, discarded Scuba diving air cylinder that had been left behind by the subterranean navigators. Also, unopened metal cans of emergency food, each can had recess in its base that contained a candle that could be removed and used to heat the contents.

And, of course, ancient footprints, left behind by those very brave scuba divers, who navigated its ancient course, to discover this wonderful cavern that can now be enjoyed by thousands of future visitors.

Having assisted with clearing the work site our plant was off hired and we lost access to the site. However, I look back at that experience that can only be achieved with participation and with happy memories, especially those miners who are probably now excavating that great tunnel in the hereafter.

Good Experience, Hard Work, and a Site left for others to enjoy.

A Passer By.

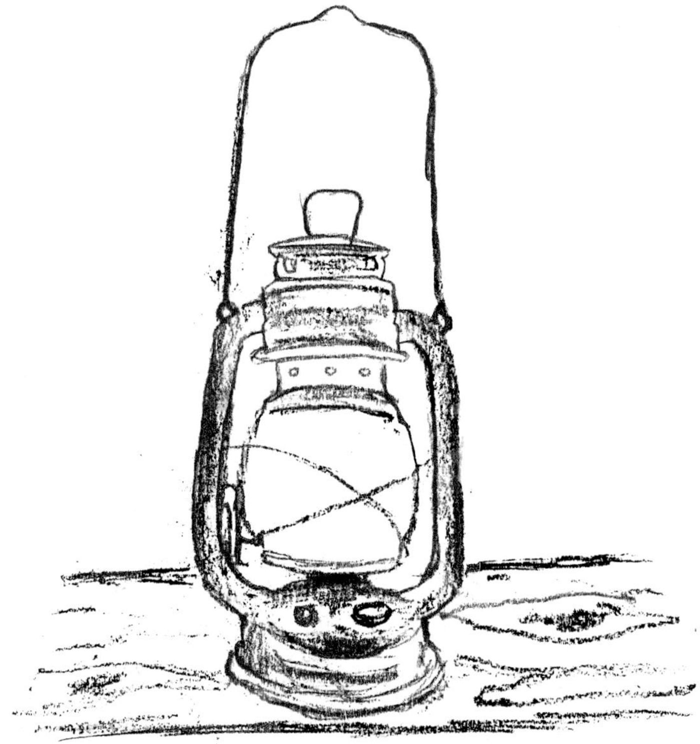

A BOY AND CIVIL DEFENCE - PART TWO

I have previously given you some idea of the instruction that myself and thousands of other volunteers underwent to prepare the country in the event of a Nuclear War. I hope you enjoy the rest of my story.

Rescue of personnel from blast damaged houses was next on my list for training and I approached this with great enthusiasm. We were instructed that the use of local materials were to be used in the event that supplied materials were not available. For instance, if there was a shortage of stretchers then the next best thing was the front door of a house or shed and after a blast there would be plenty available. The rescue lorries contained most of all the equipment required - iron bars, all needed to overcome the difficult terrain that the blast would have presented, as a challenge.

On one occasion we were instructed how to make a parallel lift from two ladders held together with rope, and with long ropes attached to each side, with this apparatus we could successfully lower a casualty on a stretcher from a bedroom window in a level, horizontal position. We were not allowed to use a real person but life-like manikins were supplied. Silence was observed during rescue operations, during which an officer would call out and we all had to listen to see if there was a response and if there was, then we had a location to which to intensify the search.

There was always hope, many houses in those days had cellars, used as a sanctuary from danger in which you would be safe and hopefully uninjured, but would have needed assistance in escaping from them due to fragments that would have fallen. Many of the instructors had gained extensive knowledge and experience from personal experience from the 2nd World War; we students looked up to them with an awe and respect that was justified. I followed all instruction with excitement and anticipation, there was no chance that my concentration would be broken by nesting magpies!

First Aid was a primary requirement and all trainees had to undergo serious instruction, lectures and practices and we spent many an hour placing bandages on fictional wounds and splints on pretend broken arms and legs.

Placing casualties in what is called the recovery position was very important for if a casualty was unconscious, then choking was a real problem if they swallowed their tongues, especially if the casualty was left unattended, awaiting collection by a field ambulance. In severe cases we were issued with large safety pins, to enable the tongue to be secured to the lip to prevent this.

Also, the placing of a ball under the arm of the casualty would suppress bleeding in the event of loss of an arm, strange but you must remember this was first response emergency treatment, all to try and keep people alive until they are transported to hospital.

It was 55 years ago that I underwent this training, and a lot of the things they taught us I have forgotten, but I'm sure a lot of it would return should the need arise.

We were taken to an old disused quarry near Weston-Super-Mare where a major disaster was re-enacted amongst all the old tin and brick sheds, including some tall stone storage towers, all of which were deemed to be on fire or full of casualties.

This was a fantastic day out and the experience gained that day will stay with me always. Of the telecommunication roll, the rescue roll, first aid and the fire fighting, I found the fire fighting the most exhilarating. The whole operation taught me leadership, compassion and responsibilities to my fellow creatures and that education will remain with me always but I'm afraid the knowledge of the great masters of literature will not.

In 1962, seven years before the SDC was stood down the Somerset branch held a huge rescue scenario in the Market Place in Wells, this was carried out by the senior fully trained operatives and instructors of the C.D.C, and I was volunteered to be a casualty. I had many injuries including a slit abdomen and missing arm, I was covered in lots a fake blood and it must have looked hideous because I can still hear the intake of the public's breath when they saw the extent of my injuries. Also, I can tell you lying on your back in the Market Place for about half an hour was uncomfortable and very cold.

The attention I received from the rescue personnel was fantastic, comforted by one person while being attended by another. I was bandaged up and removed to an awaiting ambulance. I think it was a St Johns Ambulance but not certain, anyway I was whisked away to the old WMCA Building in Chamberlain St, where volunteers supplied gallons of hot sweet tea, which was the end all of recovery remedies, in those days.

What a fantastic adventure for a young teenager.

One of the things I have not mentioned is the effect of radiation contamination; this would be the result of what is called nuclear fallout. Debris and dust created by a nuclear blast would ascend up into the atmosphere and then slowly fall back to earth. The problem was it was radioactive and was very dangerous to your health and if the wind was blowing then it would be carried a long way contaminating everything in its wake. To give you some idea, fallout from Chernobyl carried all the way to North Wales.

We were told that if you were in the path of fall-out the best place would be a nuclear bunker but these were unavailable to the general public so the next best thing was getting under the stairs in the middle of a house, especially if the house was constructed of stone and had a tiled roof, or if you had one, a cellar and stay there as long as possible or until the danger had passed.

Although the Authorities were aware of nuclear poisoning, I don't think they really had much idea how it would affect people. The magnitude of the danger came to public attention on the 26th April 1968 when the reactor at the power plant at Chernobyl blew up and caught fire. In the light of this new information I sometimes wonder whether we could have saved many lives and of course we would have put our own health a great risk, working in contaminated surroundings.

Thank God that all nations have come to their senses, and the risk of nuclear war is now almost non-existent, and long may it continue.

I left school at 16 years and went to help Dad on the farm.

Dad was one of those employers who thought, that any distraction from work, or absenteeism from the care and attention of the farm and its animals should be discouraged so we were not allowed time off for sport, or voluntary organisation. So, I regretfully handed in my resignation to the CDC and concentrated on what was now at this moment in time my future role as a dairy farmer.

The Times of Danger and Future of Peace.

A Passer By.

THE QUARRY

My next experience at quarrying came around 1972, at a different location on the Mendips; it was a small operation at a place called Leigh-on-Mendip, which is about 10 miles from Wells. The Company who operated this site was a company called Hobbs Quarries but I am unable to remember the name of this particular quarry.

The quarry produced Carboniferous Limestone, quite a common stone as found in abundance all over the Mendips. It is used mainly as a gravel as part of the ingredients of concrete manufacture also as a sub base for the construction of roadways and construction works of all kinds. It's available as large stone, small stone, gravel or dust.

I was employed at this site to load lorries for deliveries, the reason being that the Quarry's own shovel was in Tincknells of Wells for major engine rebuild.

It was an early start as the first lorry arrived to be loaded every day a 6.00 am prompt which meant I had to leave the farm at about 5.00 am. So, for a short while I was the earliest riser at home, until my Father realised this and started to rise at 4.30 am just to make sure as the Alpha Male of family he was up first. The Quarry would close at 4.30pm so it was a long day but I was young and was used to long days on the farm. It was so different from farm life, to me it was yet another great lifestyle experience that I will always remember although it was 48 years ago.

Down at the quarry bottom the stone broken down from the face by explosives was loaded onto dump trucks by two ancient Ruston Bucyrus RB10 cable operated face shovels. They were manufactured at a huge factory up in Lincoln one of the biggest manufacturers around in 1960 employing around 2000 employees.

Sometimes a stone too large for the crusher was accidentally loaded and production would come to a halt while the explosive gang blew the stone up in the crusher. The crusher was too large to be damaged but the tin roof was pitted with holes by flying splinters of rock.

The Crusher Run as it was called that spewed out of the main crusher was fed by conveyor through a secondary and then the final hammer mill, each one producing a different size product all the way down to what was called, crusher run to quarry dust.

The larger stones had to be broken down at the quarry face, a small block of explosive was places on top of each oversized rock, this was covered with a shovel of sand, to defect the blasts down into the rock, and the result was most effective.

The explosive smelt like almonds and I was told it was safe to handle but I was to wash my hands afterwards because if you did not and you touched your head or face, you would end up with a blinding headache.

The preparation for blasting at the quarry face was important, a line of blasting holes were drilled about 5m back from the work face, these were filled with sticks of explosives and the detonators connected. The siren was sounded to clear all employees from the area, the blast master pressed the plunger and the explosion brought down hundreds of tonnes to the quarry bottom ready for loading.

On the first occasion that I was involved in the blasting I was severely chastised, it all started at the explosive storage shed, the one with the sign on the entrance door that clearly said, 'danger do not enter'. The operatives loaded the entire front shovel of my machine with boxes of explosive, enough I thought to blow up Parliament. The load was indeed safe to transport, as long as, yes you have guessed it keep the detonators away at all times.

However as we progressed towards the top of the quarry with this deadly load, the operative who was responsible to carrying the detonators at a safe distance discovering that his burden was heavy decided to take a rest and placed the box of detonators on top of the boxes of explosives. I immediately knew this was wrong and brought the machine to an abrupt halt, the guy immediately realised what he had done, and quickly removed them but unfortunately for all of us it had all been witnessed by the quarry manager (enough said).

I worked at this location during January and February but went back several times later that year to carry out small excavation works. I enjoyed the experiences and the knowledge that I had experienced at that time of my youth and will always cherish the memory of the employees there who made this green-horn farmer's boy welcome and assisted with my quarrying experience and education.

Between a rock and a hard place.

A Passer By.

THE TWO COMBATANTS

The country lane was quiet, the vigorous sun shone through the lazy clouds. This was a Somerset summer at its best, all was peace in the land when all of a sudden, the two combatants fell through the hedge, one was big and one was small, each one confident that he could win the contest.

The larger one looked strong with a stocky build; he had been around, lived rough and knew how to take care of himself under all the circumstances that life threw at him, no danger of anyone taking what he wanted, when he wanted it and always well fed evidence of which was shown by the expanse of his waistline. He was a scrounger, a survivor.

The other was smaller in build, thin to look at but those muscles were hard and well used. To say he looked as if he was made of barbed wire would not be an understatement. He also knew how to take care of himself. His life was not always easy, he knew what it was like to go hungry, many days in his life he had spent not knowing where his next meal would come from, but he was also a survivor.

Both combatants had come from country families each with siblings but now found themselves trying to survive outside the comfort of the parental home, each determined to survive on their own skills and intelligence, both convinced they could make a better living than their forefathers. Survival was what they strived for, no second best for these two country rivals.

The grass and flowers that grew in the hedgerow were torn and dispersed in the wake of battle as the two of them fought through the hedgerow finally to fall into the ditch, each one trying to inflict mortal damage on the other. This was a display of hatred beyond comprehension, what was it that drove them on? Why would anyone act like this in a world of plenty, a world that should be able to dispel hatred and instil life with peace and tranquillity?

The battle continued but each now beginning to tire, one retreated and managed to climb from the ditch onto the road maybe looking for an escape route, but for some reason not taking advantage of the break in combat. The other climbed slowly from the ditch also looking tired and dishevelled but his eyes looked mean, he stared at his opponent and approached with caution. What to do next was the dilemma of the situation, back off and let peace be restored to the countryside or commit himself to a situation that could not be reversed?

The latter was the decision, and the fight broke out again, circling each other looking for the advantage trying to identify the weak points of his rival, adrenalin building up in each, driving their muscles to maximum exertions. The smaller one moved first, fast as lightning, taking his opponent with surprise but was unable to get a superior grip, he fell to one side as the other took the advantage to take command of the situation and leaped over his victim ready to inflict the final blow, but only for a moment. The small combatant knowing it was now or never used all his experience and strength, reached up and using his teeth grabbed the throat of his prey and hung on long enough to dispel all life from his victim.

So as the vigorous sun shone through the lazy clouds to alight this grisly scene, the contest was over, the Rat died, and the Weasel had his dinner.

A Passer By.

A VILLAGE ONCE KNOWN

The young girl walked up the lane from her family farm on a mission to carry out the regular request bestowed on her by her father; she passed by the home of the local dignitary the retired tea planter who had decided to live out the autumn years of his life in this lovely location.

The young girl moved on walking up the road that led to the local shop. On arrival at the counter, she pushed her father's hurried written note towards the shopkeeper who without question or enquiry handed the small girl the one large pack of cigarettes containing 100 Players Weights.

No money was exchanged as the shopkeeper put the purchase on the family account that would be settled at the end of the month. There were no questions asked as she and her family were well known by the shopkeeper, and this was a regular request. No enquiry as he knew the cigarettes would not to be distributed out to her mates or that they would be dispersed around the village, she was a trusted conveyor, and he knew her father was waiting for her.

The two village road sweepers muttered to each other as they walked through the village streets, one swept the road the other collected the sweepings and deposited them in the hedge. On many occasions he would pick up the sweepings on one side of the road and deposit them in the hedge on the opposed side of the road, strange but that was his method.

In the season they would cut back the grasses on the side of the road, clean out the drains and rod out any blockages, remove the weeds from the pavements and generally keep the village spick and span. Also, they were the purveyors of all the local news and gossip, not much happened in the village that was missed by the eagle eyes of this inquisitive duo.

Their workman rest hut was located next to the entrance gate to the field called Four Acres, situated in Middle lane, it was in here that they stored and sharpened the tools of their trade.

The farmer came around the corner on his little grey Ferguson tractor his cigarette firmly clenched in his mouth. Fixed to the back of the tractor was the link box, secured in the link box was usually his farm labourer, two milk churns, his milking equipment and feed for his cows.

He was on his way to his milking bail which was situated in the local field; there he would start the single cylinder Lister engine to power the vacuum pump.

His cows would gather around him as they knew it was milking time, also they knew that after milking they would be more comfortable. The cows would crowd to take their turns in the bail and the farmer would reward them with a few rations of cow cake. The cows would then stroll back to their feeding pastures until the next regular occasion.

The baker, the milkman, and the local coal man all made their deliveries, each knew their customers by their Christian name as new comers to the village were very rare, as each house was usually left to a family member, or purchased by a local buyer. Family names continued in the village from generation to generation and only changed if the offspring was female and the house continued in her husband's family name, or there were no children to continue the dynasty.

The elderly vicar made his way from the old vicarage which stood large and regal from its elevated site at the top of the village, he went via the footpath that crossed the stream via the old stone bridge that no one knew the age of, his journey ending at the old oak church door.

He entered and made his way to the long rope that was attached to the church bell, the appeal went out, the Faithful arrived, there to give thanks to their maker for his generosity through nature in filling the barns with hay and the larders with provisions for the winter months, and for the child that was born healthy and for the souls of the departed.

The dues were paid into the deep cloth bag that was passed around the congregation and the vicar gave out harsh warnings about what would be bestowed on the unbelievers and those who chose cider and beer, against the refreshing beverage that was the lifelong work of the retired tea planter

The faithful congregation made their way along the church path to disperse through the small gap, some to go and boil the kettle. The braver ones made their way to the local hostelry.

The old quarry worker whistled as he made his way home from the local quarry, his ancient cycle continued its reliable transport, its destiny the small cottage at the top end of the village. The bag thrown over his shoulder had contained his dinner of cheese and raw onions that had been complemented by the traditional flagon of cider.

His wife would have his tea cooking in the cast-iron range, he would just have time to weed part of his vegetable garden and feed the pig in the small sty, its destiny would be to be cured and fried for its master's future breakfast.

The landlord stood by the front door of the pub welcoming his customers with a warm handshake. Inside, his wife was busy drawing beer and cider from the many barrels that lay on the wooden support frames; in-between this she would be preparing large portions of bread and cheese, the staple menu of pubs of this era.

The customers of whom there was always many, laughed at some humorous story being told, or sympathised with someone's misfortune. The smell of beer and cider, onion and cheese, mixed with copious amounts of pipe and cigarette smoke added to the attraction of the darkened room. The guy who entered upset or sad usually left feeling elated and that his misfortune was not as bad as he originally thought, though the morning would probably tell a different story.

The sound rang out as the blacksmith from the local forge hammered out the hot steel on the century old anvil, probably one bought by his ancestors, the product brought about by hot and skilful blows would be a part for a wagon or cart, or more likely the large shoes needed for the giant shire horses that were abundant on the local farms.

He could repair the weather vane on the church tower, or refit the handle to a favourite cooking utensil, put a new handle into the staff hook, or favourite spade or shovel. Not only could he make the specialist shoes for an awkward horse's feet, but he could fit them as well as he was a skilful farrier.

Situated a safe distance away from the sparks of the forge fire stood the small hand operated petrol pump, its frequent visitors the local farmers with a request to refill the petrol tank on his tractor or fuel for the stationary engines that drove the machines in his barn or milking machine.

Is this a Village that you may know?

A Passer By.

A WALK IN THE VILLAGE

I was going for a walk, I like walking and in my younger days I walked for miles, however I have recently neglected my mobility pursuits.

A very good friend of mine said to get walking again if at all possible as it is the best remedy to rebuild neglected muscles, but to be sensible and as I have always considered myself responsible and sensible (not sure my wife would agree with that), I proceed on my mission.

The beauty of walking in the short period in Nature - that we call late winter and early spring is that the hedges have not yet regained their foliage, but there are signs that something better is on the way. This absence of foliage enables the intrepid traveller to witness hidden gems, such as the old set of horse drawn field drags that have been abandoned in the hedge by a long gone farmer never to be discovered until Nature betrays its hiding place.

I have seen old farm gates placed in a hole in the hedge as an emergency fence to hold back sheep and cattle still there many years after its valuable contribution as a farmer's aid; old pieces of galvanised tin now rusting away, anything that would act as a temporary field fencing, I suppose. All these components will stay until they completely rust away, probably not for many years to come.

In the hedge in what is now called Crossways Lane (not sure who dreamt up that gem), there is a Victorian wrought iron garden gate that has been there so long that a sapling in the hedge has captured it into its being and could only be recovered by removing the sapling, so I guess it will be there for many future years.

Have you ever noticed how long abandoned field gateways not used for years and now hidden with branches and foliage make a brief appearance at this time of winter as if to say I may have been abandoned and forgotten, but I'm still here.

Many years ago, these old entrances were blessed with fine stone gate posts, these posts were made of a conglomerate stone called locally Draycott Stone as that was where it was quarried for centuries. Sadly, most now replaced in modern gateways with wood or steel posts, I did notice some outside Stone Mead and they look fabulous and are a constant reminder of the past.

Having not walked this route for a while I notice that changes have taken place, such as a new roof on some old cottages or the repair and improvement of an untidy driveway, and what about all these solar panels? I personally do not like to see solar panels on old Victorian cottages, doesn't seem right somehow, but I guess that's the future and many will disagree with my opinions, I don't want people to be upset by my opinions.

Well what about all these new road signs? What's that all about, I wonder? I don't know how I have managed to navigate the village and find people's houses in the last 50 years of wandering the village. As far as I'm concerned, their appearance implies that this wonderful historic village has been transformed by someone into what might by some locals, be described as a Millennial modified Borough. I was once told that signs were for the abeyance of fools and guidance of wise men, but of course that's not my opinion, but it might come close.

We have a lot of dog walkers in the village and I do not have a problem with that, dogs are good company and I enjoy the company of my grandchildren's dogs, also if you have a dog it will encourage you to walk, and as I said, walking is good.

Responsible owners clear up after their pets and that is to be encouraged and I was pleased to see the new disposal bin being placed outside Browne's Hayes field. The problem is as its about five feet off the ground, how do elderly owners manage to lift their large dogs that high so that the dog can relieve itself in the bin? I may have got that wrong, but you have to have a sense of humour.

Its current site is a bit intrusive as it is right in your face as you enter the village, could it not be better placed on a more camouflaged site? It will make the village tidier, and anyway do we need two bins within 100 metres of each other? There was already one positioned at the entrance of the Crossways Inn car park.

I have noticed that since the new houses have been built

opposite the Crossways that a large amount of ground water now runs down the surface of the road, this is not good especially if it freezes. It never used to do that, I'm sure this could be addressed by the people in power, but as it's been a problem for a long time now, I guess people in power have not noticed it or do not rate it as a serious problem.

I also see there is a small building being constructed in the Crossways car park. It will be interesting to know its future use, or am I just being nosy?

It is nice to see the Churchyard nice and tidy again and I do admire the volunteers who give up their valuable free time to assist in keeping it so. I hope they don't remove the old gravestones to make maintenance easier, some churches have done that but thank goodness, not ours.

I wonder what happened last summer, why was it allowed to rewild? It did really look untidy, perhaps experiments have to take place so we can learn lessons, please let's keep it tidy in respect for those that rest there, especially as it designated a Commonwealth War Graveyard and this alone must be respected as I know it is by the whole village.

I have never seen so much Mistletoe that has established in many of the local trees, if you own a tree with this parasite living off it, destroy it before it destroys your tree, believe me if the mistletoe wins the day the tree will surely die tomorrow.

We have problems with Ash dieback, and I'm afraid it will destroy many of our lovely ash trees, there is no known cure for this infestation at this moment in time, so to try and contain the disease we have to cut down and remove them. Some owners are pollarding the tree as an experiment toward a cure, the only good news is that Ash makes wonderful firewood, not much use to those of you without fireplaces.

I have seen the advert, that we have saw mill in the village called Dangerous Dave, I think that describes the name given to the saw, and not the operator. I know him and I have every confidence he is up to speed with health and safety issues and is a skilled and competent operative.

Oh, I may take my next dead ash tree to him to be milled, it should produce some useful timber. Making use of local trees for construction within the confines of the village must tick all the environmental boxes.

A village revisited.

(May I take this opportunity to wish you all a Merry Christmas, and prosperous New Year).

A Passer By.